AWAKENING
THE OTHER WAY

Cover photography: Eva Bronzini (2021), *Brown Rope on White Surface*.

Marcel Eschauzier

AWAKENING
THE OTHER WAY

Nonduality and Existential Reason

BRUSSELS
XRLMEDIA
2023

Copyright © 2023 Marcel Eschauzier
All rights reserved. No part of this book may be reproduced or used in any matter without the written permission of the copyright owner except for the use of quotations in a book review.
Some characters in this book are inspired by actual and historical persons but are not intended to represent these persons or their views accurately. They are merely imagined by the author for philosophical purposes.
ASIN B0C7H7TN48 (ebook)
ISBN 979-8397544009 (paperback)
ISBN 979-8397596244 (hardcover)

"There is nothing wrong with thinking, but don't forget to feel."

—César Millán

CONTENTS

PROLOGUE
1. HOW I AWAKENED ... 1
   Of theory and practice ... 6
   Of seekers and finders ... 11
   Epicurus explains ... 15
2. AWAKENING AND THE RESULTING MINDSET ... 18
   Metaphysics ... 28
   The enlightenment experience ... 34
   The enlightened mindset ... 45
   Epicurus meets Einstein ... 52
3. NONDUALITY AND REASON ... 57
   Existential reason ... 67
   The tree ... 76
   Epicurus meets Lao Tzu ... 83
4. THE NATURE OF OUR NONDUALITY ... 87

The false promise of mind transcendence	90
Nonduality and virtue	98
The way of our nondual hearts	107
Common objections to nondualism	121
Epicurus meets Sam Harris	125
The Zen master	130

PROLOGUE

"*Hey.*"

"Hey. Who are you?"

"*I'm Epicurus.*"

"The illustrious Greek thinker who lived around 300 BCE, founder of the Epicureanism philosophy? Who advocated simple pleasures, fearlessness of the gods, and friendship? Whose school welcomed women and men, free and enslaved? No way!"

"*Yes way!*"

"Oh, I get it. You only exist in my imagination."

"*That's right.*"

"Still, I'm honored and thrilled to meet you in person. You're a unique teacher. In this book, I want to introduce more exceptional thinkers like yourself. Maybe you could have a word with them to clarify some misunderstandings about your philosophy?"

"*Let's see what you're writing. 'Awakening the Other Way.' You can read that in two ways, right? Awakening as a noun or verb.*"

"Way to go, Epicurus! They already told me you were perceptive—an ace at reason."

"*Oh, don't be silly.... But how do you reckon I fit in with your book? Is it supposed to be a guide?*"

"Good philosophy like yours gives guidance in life."

"I agree. But awakening... They told me that you can get neurotic sometimes. Are you really a Zen person?"

"You are true to your reputation, Epicurus; you don't mince words! Neurotic... I prefer tenacious. Impatient. It helps me with writing books, though. I can get lost in thought. If I wouldn't also be, uh... *passionate* about my work, I'd lose my thread and never finish."

"You're like a medical doctor who smokes."

"Maybe I am, Epicurus. I am not a spiritual teacher like Eckhart Tolle or Sam Harris. The best spiritual teachers lead by example, which is why I learned so much from these gentlemen. But we also have our differences of opinion. Would you mind if I introduce you to Sam Harris later? I'd love to have your view."

"Sure, why not."

"Thanks, Epicurus. My role is different from theirs. I am not a spiritual teacher but an engineer who likes philosophy and had the good fortune of being touched by nondualistic insight. I didn't come across a satisfactory explanation of nondualistic metaphysics, while it can help spiritual seekers so much. Once they get it, most are smart enough to apply it to their lives without my spiritual guidance."

"You mean that not all enlightened people are spiritual teachers? Just like not all spiritual teachers are enlightened? Makes sense."

"Uncanny... it's almost unreal how well you understand me! And about my impatience, I believe being passionate is compatible with nondualistic awareness."

"So you don't always have peace of mind but still have something to share?"

"Right. Enlightened people must still grapple with human issues—as long as we don't consider them super-human. The enlightened mind is just better equipped to cope with them. So, it seems to me that an informed, genuinely human philosophy includes both accurate nondualistic metaphysics *and* the passions. Can we still call it truly nondualistic if it doesn't? Don't you think enlightened people can get excited and upset too?"

PROLOGUE

"It depends on what you mean by enlightened."

"I mean people who have grasped nondualistic metaphysics: that the mind and the rest of the world are one, and what that means for our lives."

"Not sure I follow you. The mind must be part of the physical body. How else could they interact?"

"O, Epicurus, you hit the nail on the head! But Plato and many other iconic Western thinkers consider the immaterial mind separate from the material world. Otherwise, they argue, the world must disappear when we go to sleep or even blink our eyes. Even Einstein finds it obvious that the moon still exists when we don't look at it. Most people still believe in a mind-independent physical reality because evolution has cut out our minds to conceive her. But no one can explain *how* the material world interacts with the immaterial mind."

"Are you saying I'm enlightened?"

"You are close because you realize that the mind and physical world must be one. But how do you explain to someone like Einstein that the moon doesn't disappear when he is sleeping? If you solve this riddle, you are without a doubt enlightened. The problem is that the solution is so counterintuitive that the human mind almost automatically rejects it before it can even consider it."

"What is it then?"

"In *Chapter 3*, you will meet Lao Tzu. He already solved the riddle two-and-a-half thousand years ago. Few understand the relationship between the mind and the rest of the world. Yet it is perhaps *the* key issue in psychology, physics, and ethics."

"But what does it bring when you can still get neurotic—uhm, sorry . . . impatient—like you? Isn't your enlightenment just a word game?"

"You won't always have peace of mind, but you will be connected with the sublime present, which gives you instant *access* to inner peace and truth. It will give you everything you need, and you can also simply marvel at it for its own sake. When you have found that truth and learned how to rely on it, life's trials and tribulations become more of an exciting adventure and less of an endless torment. Anyway, Epicurus, do you truly believe people always want peace of mind? Will that make them happy?"

"*Peace of mind is delightful but not the only pleasure there is. Life is also an adventure to share and enjoy. By the way, how did you get to know me?*"

"Once upon a time, when we were still roaming the globe, my friend Bernhard talked about you. He told me you said it's okay to pursue pleasures. And that the pleasures of the body can be replaced by the pleasures of the soul when one gets older. It seemed a plainspoken but truthful message—and hopeful as well because most of us hope to achieve old age."

"*Aha! Now I see why you like my philosophy. You are an egoistic hedonist!*"

"You make it sound terrible, Epicurus. And it's *your* philosophy."

"*Right. The first impression of my teachings isn't always favorable because they don't sound all that nice. Still, they are true.*"

"Maybe that's why I like you. You see what drives people to virtue or vice for what it is: whatever people value—for themselves. Altruism is the product of a noble but ultimately egoistic mind. Perhaps it's my Dutch cultural background: We like straight shooting. But others often perceive us as rude."

"*Sounds familiar. But pleasures, for me, are simple pleasures like friendship. Not vain ones like power, status, fame, and wealth because they can never be completely satisfied. And tranquility, inner peace is the highest pleasure.*"

"I feel you."

"*And if there is no higher truth than the mind, as you nondualists allege, then it is only sincere to admit that pleasure, or more simply put, human value, is the guiding force of our behavior, rather than being virtuous in the eyes of otherworldly powers. We will never know the likes and dislikes of supernatural beings as long as we admit that we are merely human. And that's okay. Virtue is born of wisdom and understanding the misery of toxic desires rather than the naive belief that it is automatically rewarded.*"

"You and I have a lot to talk about."

1
HOW I AWAKENED

December 31, 1989. A new decade dawns. I hope it will be better than the eighties because I cannot go on this way. Ever since adolescence, I've been depressed. I don't see a way out. At the height of my despair, a thought comes to my mind: *If I, for a moment, forget all my failures, weaknesses, and anger, all the negatives past and future, then I am still alive but suddenly open to the world without any weight on my shoulders. What if everything is nothing? Then I am still here but now totally free. The world keeps on turning but is suddenly okay because when I look at where my problems were . . . they are gone!*

And just like that, I have overcome my depression. I am nineteen years old when I find a place of peace inside myself that makes me courageous, adventurous, *alive*. My self-pity and self-doubt are gone. Ever since, I know how to stop worrying too much, for example, about what people think of me. I remember that night crashing a New Year's party with some friends, having the time of our lives. The next day, I arrive at the traditional New Year's Day family meeting. I still hear *Technotronic's Pump Up the Jam* inside my foggy head when I utter a good morning. My family looks worried since it's already four in the afternoon. I don't recommend excesses or crashing parties, but neither do I regret that night's celebration.

Later, I shape my insight into a mantra: "Nothing."[1] Whenever I need it, I repeat this mantra to myself. It immediately releases me from my fears and problems and just freely lets me be and do. The "nothingness" isn't cynical or conscienceless; it merely liberates my mind from superfluous burdens. When I say "nothing" to myself, I remind myself of what it's really all about: living, being in the present. *Everything is nothing, and nothing is everything is the truth.* "Nothing," you live now, and it's okay. Finally, my life takes off, and I spend the next 28 years traveling the world and making many dreams come true.

During this happy chapter of my life, I remain oblivious that I have established contact with the *nonduality* through my mantra. I wouldn't consider myself awakened, though, since I haven't yet grasped nondualistic metaphysics.

※

Summer 2016. I may have exaggerated my celebration of life and freedom. I am 47 years old when I experience a "reverse midlife crisis." While some guys feel "trapped" at this age, longing for more freedom, I realize instead that I miss having a home and family of my own.

My friend Theo and I are on a road trip from Bucharest to Brussels, and we stop over in Brno, Czech Republic. There, we are sitting on the roadside, eating a burger, when I suddenly become aware of the hollowness (emptiness, but not in the good sense) of my life and start sobbing. Admittedly, my sentimental mood is fueled by the superb Czech beers, but it feels miserable all the same. Theo consoles me. But I know now that I must liberate myself again—this time from foolishly following my zest for freedom. I have to make a change in my life. But how can I let go of the freedom I love so much?

---

[1] In my native Dutch "niets," a for a mantra convenient one-syllable word.

1. HOW I AWAKENED

Later that year, my search for answers by studying philosophy and psychology intensifies. My alternating yearning for freedom and belonging reaches a fever pitch. Then I come across Alan Watts's 1957 *The Way of Zen* and his other material. Some wheels inside my head suddenly come to a grinding halt . . . and are reversed. *What if . . . ? Why didn't I see this before? Of course! The answer is right there! All the answers are right there!* On a Sunday morning on my bachelor pad's balcony, I awaken.

It is as if something flicks a switch, suddenly illuminating the dark corners of my mind. Right there and then, I know that I have been looking for answers in all the wrong places and that the right place is so close to me that it has always eluded me. The undoubtable source of truth reveals itself to me. It is the being before any question can be formulated, the being in which right and wrong are not yet divided. It is the all-encompassing present that is existence itself.

Only later do I find the terms to describe my experience of insight. Satori, finding Tao, awakening to the nondual presence. Other applicable words are absolute clarity, pure truth, profound inner peace, coming home, and the birth of an inner smile that has accompanied me ever since.

More practically speaking, it also gives me the courage to propose to my longtime girlfriend and partner—who, to my great delight, dares to take the plunge with me. Earlier, my fear of commitment, amplified by an admittedly immature feeling of missing out on a happy adolescence, prevented me from doing so.

Before my awakening, I was convinced that there was always a right and a wrong way of doing things, and I had a hard time accepting the downside of any of my decisions. I saw them as my failures. Now that I am awakened, I understand why my perfectionism was a mistake. No decision or action can ever be perfect because the worlds we *conceive* are always imperfect. However, they don't have to be perfect because . . . they don't exist!

Instead, one can turn to the present for answers. Our

present being is always whole because it precedes the imagined distinction between right and wrong. So, for one's decisions, one shouldn't seek perfection but follow the present's undivided truth, which is the same as the way of the heart. Perfection is an illusion but love an essence.

It makes me realize I don't want to go through life without my partner and soon-to-be wife. I have come to terms with the altogether common need to close some doors to pass through new ones. We settle down near Brussels in Belgium.

❈

Fall 2022. I have given up my globetrotting consultant life and am writing books instead. After publishing my third book about nonduality, I am enjoying a break. My mind exits the tunnel I confined it to while writing. I turn my attention to the outside world with what feels like a more comprehensive understanding of nonduality.

Writing is highly instructive as it reveals contradictions. You may think you understand something, but when you have to write it down, you often discover that you don't. Countless times, I had to do more research and "go back to the drawing board" when I found inconsistencies in my comprehension of the nonduality I had so doubtlessly experienced or had deeper insights into it. Early on, the world teaches engineers like me that the devil is always in the details. When you overlook small design flaws, they usually come back to bite you. So often, I had to rebuild my framework of thinking about nonduality—until it had become consistent, robust, and reliable.

Looking around me outside "the tunnel," I am struck by a few particularities of nonduality that didn't catch my attention before:
- ✓ Although enlightenment is not conceptual, it is helpful to conceptualize the experience to understand and explain it. Nondualists prefer not to make an enemy of their own thinking because they want to avoid splitting

1. HOW I AWAKENED

their mind into rival parts. Enlightenment is non-conceptual, but so is the smell of a rose, and it would be a sad world if we weren't supposed to think or write about it.
- ✓ If you cannot explain enlightenment to people open to it, you probably don't understand it well enough.
- ✓ Many people don't *want* to understand nonduality and never will. They often prefer a faith-based worldview and have the amazing ability to filter out the facts and evidence that don't support it. This observation is not a reproach. Nonduality's full breadth can be dazzling and intimidating. We are human, not logical computers, so I have no business telling others what to believe.

During my break, I do some reading. My interpretation of nonduality is entirely rooted in my own experience—as it should be because one can only understand it from a first-person viewpoint—but I am curious about the material of other authors, thinkers, spiritual teachers, and mindfulness meditation coaches. My enlightenment followed metaphysical insight. Another path is through spiritual practice. I want to explore such spiritual experiences and discover how they can help me become more patient.

I explore modern guided meditation. During earlier experiments with more traditional zazen (sitting) meditation, I experienced astounding feelings I want to learn more about. I read about Stoicism—not a nondualistic philosophy but fascinating all the same. I familiarize myself with the teachings of the famous spiritual master Eckhart Tolle. And I get acquainted with some of the many Indian gurus who have taught nondualism to the West.

While learning about spirituality and equanimity, I also notice that I have something to share and contribute about nonduality. The spiritual teachers and thinkers I come across didn't achieve their enlightenment predominantly through metaphysical insight as I did. Theirs was a path of spiritual experience. Some seem unsure if they found the nonduality—

a telling sign they didn't. I also stumble upon inconsistencies in the enlightenment interpretations of the type I had to reject during my earlier attempts to explain my awakening. Other interpretations are spot on but can still be massively simplified. At the same time, I get inspired by the spontaneity of what I read and realize that I could make my insights easier to digest by telling a more personal story—something I mostly shied away from. As a result, I soon find myself working again—on the book you are reading now.

OF THEORY AND PRACTICE

I lack patience. Not that I am proud of it or don't want to do something about it, but I just have to admit that I don't possess this precious quality. I get pushy when I feel something needs to be done. Fortunately for myself and perhaps the people around me, I have a mental "trick" at my disposal. I can instantly mentally connect with the nonduality ("Tao") and snap out of my hang-ups. This connection has become so ubiquitous in my mind that I consider it part of me. Deep down, I remain at peace even when I worry about something.

Enlightenment is a loaded word. But if we define it in a metaphysical sense as *satori* and *finding Tao*—I will explain later what that means—then, thankfully, I may consider that it has been given to me. Enlightenment can be reached via spiritual practice, like meditation, or directly via metaphysical insight. I still have much to learn about spirituality and find solace in the material of the many exceptional spiritual teachers, past and present. They help me become more equanimous.

I can almost hear you ask, "How can you call yourself enlightened when you still want to become more patient?" Enlightenment is generally considered something that leads to serenity, contentment, and magnanimity. While I agree that it contributes tremendously to them, equating such virtues with

1. HOW I AWAKENED

enlightenment is a mistake. Sometimes, an enlightened person can still feel miserable, be grumpy, nervous, and even unkind. Another choice of words might make this statement more palatable: how about being passionate about something or someone? You may agree that true passion can make one exceedingly needy and volatile. Should an enlightened person, therefore, quell passions and let purposefulness, burning love, and determination be things of the past? I don't think so!

Many spiritual teachers—especially contemporary ones—encourage virtue to achieve enlightenment and promise well-being in return. Criticizing this approach is perilous for those who don't want to be branded a cynic. I am a staunch supporter of virtue, kindness, and well-being, so I hope to avoid this label. Still, let me propose a short fictional story as a thought experiment to test the validity of equating enlightenment with serenity, magnanimity, or well-being.

> On a starry summer night, a famous enlightened spiritual teacher named Alice walks into a beachfront bar. There are two other guests: a handsome man and an attractive woman. The spiritual teacher recognizes the guy as Bob, her high school crush. Alice is single, and seeing Bob rekindles strong feelings. She instantly hopes to leave with him for a romantic walk on the moonlit beach. However, the attractive woman has also set her eyes on Bob as she is obviously flirting. Alice is wise indeed but also human and can't help but feel a pang of jealousy. She is an expert in mastering her feelings and has no problem hiding them.
> The attractive lady, who introduces herself as Claire, recognizes the famous Alice. She whispers in her ear, "I'm a big fan of yours; hopefully, you can tell me what to do.... I am still married, but my husband is unfaithful, and we will soon divorce. Bob and I have such great chemistry! I want to invite him for a beach walk with me, Alice! Should I do it?"
> Alice wonders... Should she be magnanimous and

kind and encourage Bob and Claire to take off together, losing her opportunity to catch up with Bob? Or should she listen to her strong feelings and remind Claire of her wedding vows despite Claire's husband's infidelity?

The story doesn't tell what Alice does next. I'm not a relationship expert, so I also cannot tell you what Alice should do, except that I hope she follows her heart. But we notice that if Alice doesn't fight her desires, she has to choose between hurting Claire's feelings and possibly feeling guilty or sacrificing her own. She could also consider Bob's sentiments and reckon she has more to offer than Claire. But would Claire agree in that case?

In life, we are sometimes suspended between guilt and grief, as but one of the feeling polarities that energize our thoughts and actions.[2] This is even the case for enlightened persons—especially those frequenting bars. The problem with philosophical or spiritual systems that demand virtue is that they ignore that in life, not all situations are *win-win*—even though most are, making them always worthy of pursuit. Sometimes, one's virtue comes at the expense of someone else. A philosophical implication of nondualism is that there is no such thing as an absolute virtue.

Spiritual teachers' emphasis on specific virtues has more philosophical issues. Many recommend thinking less and feeling more. But should we criticize someone for enjoying complex literature or playing chess? Others advise us to *slow down* and not be hurried anymore. Thus, we are supposed to better savor the moment. It is indeed delightful to unwind. But how about an athlete sprinting to Olympic gold? Isn't it possible to savor the moment when one does something fast?

---

[2] The human conscious mind is built on inner conflict. If navigating inner conflicts didn't create biological value for our species, evolution would have only endowed us with instinctive and reflexive behavior.

And is it truly always best for us to "be in the moment?" How about when you're at the dentist's having a root canal? Is it wrong to want to *escape* such a moment and imagine being on a beautiful beach instead?

Then there is the frequent advice to stop worrying and overthinking and to put more trust in one's feelings and "the universe." This sounds like superb advice, but as always, the devil is in the details. Anyone who has ever done something rather complex—so, mostly everyone—knows that many things can go terribly wrong without proper preparation.

So, if not virtue, at least not directly, then what *does* a spiritual teacher have to offer? Many pledge an awakening of nondualistic awareness via spiritual practice like meditation. Since I awakened through metaphysical insight instead of spiritual practice, I cannot comment on that. One can awaken only once. The main benefit of spiritual practice for me is simply well-being. It is an ever-relevant reminder not to get stuck in the conceptual worlds the mind creates and to allow it to connect with the nondual realms of the present instead.

Why, then, did I write this book while there are already so many outstanding ones about awakening to the nonduality? Because I didn't find any that adequately clarifies the awakening via metaphysical insight as I experienced it. The path via metaphysical insight seems atypical, even though it is easier to explain. The "metaphysical" approach, compared to the "spiritual," relies more on the precision of words. For straightforward reasons that we will see, the nonduality itself cannot be conceived or put into words. Yet, all communication—even nonverbal—relies on concepts. More precise language dramatically reduces confusion about an already challenging topic.

I hold that awakening by metaphysical insight has at least the same positive effects on virtue and mental well-being as awakening by spiritual practice. For example, improved existential understanding enhances your ability to recognize and deal with toxic desires that may otherwise lead to vice and misery.

A thorough grasp of the human mind's "place" in the nonduality adds the benefit that it so deeply corrects your understanding of our world that it is immediately ingrained. A true awakening through metaphysical insight leaves the mind no choice but to stay sufficiently in touch with the nonduality. Once understood, you can also better recognize false awakenings—for example, when confused with mere virtue or blissful spiritual feelings.

Moreover, once you understand nondualistic metaphysics, you do not doubt the oneness of the "spiritual" and "rest of" the world. This increases the scope of nondual awareness spectacularly: from merely spirituality to literally everything. Many nondualism teachers call for more nondualistic awareness in worldly affairs. Enlightenment by metaphysical insight answers such calls.

In this book, I invite you to discover nondualistic metaphysics and join me on an expedition into the mind and our shared existence. I hope you will enjoy it and that serious and not-so-serious thinkers and seekers find something useful for their journey.

But there is more to this book. Nondualism implies that philosophy may be judged by its usefulness because truth and human value coincide in our nondual essence. Perhaps the best way to understand the urgency of sound philosophy is by reading the news. As a concerned citizen, I will discuss the current Western thought crisis, which I blame on *secular dualism*. We distrust subjectivity even though we cannot escape it. Our misguided faith in *reality* comes at the expense of *reason* and has left the West confused and vulnerable.

Some see the same problem and plea for a return to religious dualism. I don't, even though I treasure the Catholic tradition I grew up in. Instead, I explain how existential reason, which is rational thought rooted in our inevitable subjectivity, can be applied to individual and collective existential issues. Nondualism brings back common sense in the public arena

1. HOW I AWAKENED

because it allows us to reasonably judge. Existential reason is also compatible with religious beliefs because it only concerns everything human.

Nondualism entails that entirely objective observers cannot exist. Accordingly, my viewpoints on various societal issues shine through. You may not agree with me, and that's okay because I don't have all the answers. The issues and my arguments are intended to illustrate how nondualism and existential reason permit a civic and solution-driven dialogue about our collective challenges.

OF SEEKERS AND FINDERS

Just like one cannot be a little bit pregnant, one cannot be a little bit enlightened. Enlightenment is a binary state of mind: You have it or you don't. This state of mind isn't based on faith—a belief without justification or on utilitarian grounds—but on the perfectly sensible insight that duality is an illusion and the deep understanding of what that means.

Being enlightened frees you from lots of suffering that you unknowingly, incessantly, and unnecessarily create for yourself. But enlightenment doesn't turn you into a different person. It doesn't change you into an angelic creature, eternally blissful and above inner conflict and pain. It doesn't transform you into a perfectly virtuous saint or an all-knowing sage. Enlightenment is in every respect entirely human.

Enlightenment doesn't automatically make one wise[3], and many unenlightened people are wiser than enlightened ones. Much of the wisdom associated with enlightenment is also available to unenlightened people. Even commonplace advice, such as seizing the day, enjoying the little things in life, and

---

[3] I eat pizza with pineapple.

remembering our mortality, drives at awareness of the present miracle. Enlightenment merely helps you see the big picture of such advice and clarifies *how* to be more present.

Before I started writing about nonduality, I was a business consultant. Like many in business, I took a fair number of management courses. In one of them, the teacher presented a four-phase model of learning a skill—any skill. Business people love quadrant models, and I won't trouble you more than necessary with this one. But the teacher made several points that stuck with me and also apply to spiritual seeking.

Enlightenment isn't an acquired skill but an insight that has to be received. However, preparing the mind for receiving this insight *is* an acquirable skill: the skill that Zen monks develop on their way to *satori*. Satori is the moment one fathoms the dualistic illusion.

The four-stage model went like this: Imagine you have to learn a new skill, like flying a helicopter. Let's assume that you, just like me, don't know how to do that. In the first learning phase, you are aware that you cannot fly the helicopter.

After a great deal of training, you start to know how to maneuver the craft. In your enthusiasm, you may overestimate your abilities. This second learning phase is risky because you're unaware you aren't yet fully capable of flying the helicopter. There is a parallel here with spiritual seekers who have their first spiritual experiences. They are understandably excited and want to share their findings. But because of their limited grasp, they aren't yet ready to deal with the harsh skepticism of the outside world. So, it's helpful to take your time and remain modest and curious in spiritual matters. Remember, enlightenment is not about arriving somewhere but finding what you look for in your journey.

In the third phase of learning how to fly a helicopter, you have done the hard work of training but aren't yet aware that you have become proficient. In this phase, your confidence lags behind your skills. In terms of enlightenment, seekers may have unknowingly established contact with the nonduality. I remained at this stage for 28 years. I used my "nothing" mantra to mentally merge with the present but was still unaware that I had stumbled upon something known as Tao. I didn't even consider myself a spiritual seeker.

The takeaway is that you can acquire existential wisdom in numerous ways, not only through spiritual practice geared toward enlightenment. Enlightenment always eludes you when you chase after it. It may come unexpectedly to you when all your useful but seemingly unrelated abilities and knowledge suddenly *connect*, and you find yourself already much more accomplished than you thought you were.

In the fourth learning phase, you are aware of your proficiency in piloting the helicopter and have a realistic view of the extent and limitations of your skills. But, as the course teacher taught us, even a proud phase-four helicopter pilot is still only in phase one, two, or three of learning other skills. In our complex world, it is impossible to master everything. Even the most capable, seasoned master in one domain is still a learner in others.

Enlightenment itself is not a skill. It is a mindset and deep conviction resulting from a mind-bending but fact-based insight. So, there aren't four phases to achieve it. However, the depth of *understanding* enlightenment and its benefits *is* subject to learning and improvement. Since enlightenment is an insight, one can get it only once. Some have achieved enlightenment through spiritual practice and are experts in spiritual experience. Others are teaching experts. Still others— like me—have achieved enlightenment via metaphysical insight but have little experience in spiritual practice and teaching. Although I am a finder of enlightened metaphysics and relish the inner peace it brings, I remain a seeker in other fields.

As will become clear, the Tao is a "familiar mystery" from which you and I are not separate. Enlightened people may be satisfied with their existential answers but still cannot avoid all troubles in life. No matter how impressive your existential insights and spiritual skills are, you still have to cope with human challenges and the circumstance of being born into a mystery without asking for it. Fortunately, we have each other to help make sense of our existence and give meaning to it. Sometimes teachers need students as much as students need teachers.

Since nondualism is always about the road and not the goal, it seems okay that even those with something to share and teach remain simultaneously seekers in other fields. In a nondual world, mere mortals like (most of) us don't just sit and radiate pure wisdom permeating the students' souls. True nondualism is never about the supernatural but always about the miracle of being truly human. The supernatural is separate from our nature, so not human and intrinsically dualistic.

It is in this spirit of learning and deep respect that I compare my nondualistic understanding with the metaphysics of others: Eckhart Tolle, the spiritual teacher and author of the 1997 bestselling book *The Power of Now*, Sam Harris, the bestselling author, philosopher, neuroscientist, and creator of the meditation course app *Waking Up*, and the greatest genius of the modern times, Albert Einstein, who happened to be a declared dualist. If I didn't feel I had something to add to their views, each a thought leader in their field, this book wouldn't have served a purpose, and I wouldn't have written it.

I particularly examine Eckhart Tolle's outlook. His approach to the nonduality via spiritual experience differs from mine via metaphysical insight. This offers a splendid opportunity to bridge the divide between spirituality on the one hand and science and reason on the other, as true nondualism demands. The depth of his spiritual understanding, renown, and outspokenness help me clarify various points.

In 2021, a reviewer of my first book—a philosophical deep-dive called *Existential Rationalism*—pointed out that I could reach a wider audience by writing in a less technical, friendlier way: like Eckhart Tolle. At that time, I didn't know him, which shows how spiritually under-read I am. My views on nonduality are rooted in my own experience. Before writing this book, I finally found the time to explore Tolle's work.

For the few who don't know him either, Tolle, German-born, is an enlightened spiritual teacher. His bestselling books and other material have inspired millions to get in touch with "the Now." Tolle's charismatic, diminutively humorous, and utterly calm bearing is a wonderful example of how great teachers communicate nonverbally and lead by example. Merely hearing and seeing him speak on YouTube helped me feel more calm and patient.

In *The Power of Now*, he unambiguously answers many student questions. The certainty he encounters in the nondual present is reflected in his work. Tolle achieved enlightenment through spiritual experience. In 1977, when he was 29 years old, he had an overwhelming and compelling spiritual experience of connecting to the nonduality ("Being" in his words).

Compared to my first step toward awakening at age 19 and my satori and finding Tao experiences at age 47, his was more radical and influenced his life more drastically. After the event, he became a spiritual teacher. From what he says, I am convinced that the nonduality he speaks of is the same as I found, even though his spiritual approach differs considerably from mine.

EPICURUS EXPLAINS

"So, this is your first chapter?"

"Yes, Epicurus. It's a bit uncomfortable for introverts like me to share personal spiritual moments. But I want this book to be more relatable than my previous ones."

"Ha! You don't strike me as an introvert when you write like that. You flaunt your feelings in search of sympathy!"

"Oops... do you think so? Maybe I do. It's not indispensable but nice to find a sympathetic ear. Who doesn't want to be heard?"

"Well, Stoics teach that you shouldn't aim for such vanities as sympathy and recognition. It's best to have low expectations."

"That sounds smart. So do they say it's better to please yourself than others?"

"In a way, yes—but Stoics prefer calling it 'being virtuous' instead of 'pleasing themselves.' Stoics and Epicureans are often considered on the opposite side of a spectrum. According to the stereotypes, Stoics suppress their desires to find equanimity, while Epicureans follow their desires. But Stoics know that not all desires are bad and Epicureans that not all desires are good, so there is a reasonable middle ground between them. Did you know that the famous Stoic Seneca praised the effects of wine on inner peace?"

"Is that so? Still, Epicurus, you philosophers are good in theory, but in practice, people *do* have passions and desires even when they aren't always perfectly reasonable. It's precisely what makes passions out of desires—and us human to have them. Passions aren't within our control because they arise spontaneously."

"*But your beliefs profoundly influence your passions. And your beliefs* are *within your control. You can correct harmful beliefs.*"

"How do you do that, Epicurus?"

"*That's our ancient-Greek specialty! We invented* reason *for that.*"

"I see. So, you wouldn't mind discussing *reason* in the next chapter with a special guest?"

"*Who is it?*"

"Albert Einstein, the greatest thinker of our times. Something like Plato in your time."

"*Oh no, not Plato! He's a genius, but I don't quite follow his metaphysics.*"

"Einstein is a genius like Plato, and both have similar metaphysical ideas. They are dualistic—so I was hoping you'd have a word with him, using that specialty of yours: reason."

"*Sure, why not. I wonder what our offspring have come up with after more than two thousand years of Western metaphysics. Maybe I'll*" *understand it better then. Plato confuses me. He wrote dialogues of Socrates to get his points across, so I'm not always sure what his own views are. It's a clever rhetorical technique, though."*

"Don't give me ideas. . . ."

2

AWAKENING AND THE RESULTING MINDSET

There are many reasons to mystify enlightenment. One of them is that it indeed involves a mystery: a technical hard limit of what concepts can convey. A second is that one cannot explain more than one understands. And I must even mention a third reason: Some say they have access to mystical realms beyond the human mind, where spiritual treasures abound. Their claims enable them to mesmerize a following and find fame and fortune.

What could motivate me to *demystify* enlightenment? First of all, a genuine wish to share my insights. Improved metaphysical understanding can help people individually and collectively in all sorts of ways. It's a central theme of my writing. But don't let anyone fool you, also not me. Of course, I also hope that my work will be read. I am human and don't consider vanity beyond me.

Generally speaking, I feel we shouldn't always condemn human weaknesses when they do little harm and contribute to "worthy causes." How foolish (and vain!) are those who declare themselves above their humanity! Our strong desire to

2. AWAKENING AND THE RESULTING MINDSET

escape our humanity, to *transcend* our being, makes us an eager audience of those claiming to know how to do that.

But let me tell you a little secret: True enlightenment is *not* transcendence of your being. It is *not* about being perfectly virtuous and above all human weaknesses. It is *not* about becoming omniscient, angelically serene, and perfectly calm no matter the circumstances. Because as long as you look for the truth outside of your humanity, it will always escape you. It is like chasing your tail.

Instead, the nondualistic truth can be found *within* yourself. Let's start by briefly exploring this *inner truth*. The first simple observation you can make about your inner truth is that you *know* what it feels like. When you are told a profound truth, it feels different from an outright lie. But when you are aware of being lied to, you also *know* that it is the case. All feelings of knowing, but also all other feelings and perceptions, have something in common. What they have in common is a root sense of knowing. This root sense of knowing before you know *what* you know, feel, or perceive is your inner truth. It is that simple.

I will explain a lot more about inner truth, but if you, just now, could recognize your inner truth, you may want to make a mental note. Because with everything you're going to read and hear from me and others, and all that you will say to yourself, it is extremely easy to lose sight of your inner truth. Inner truth is so easy to overlook that most people never notice it *during their entire lives*. If you, just now, could sense your inner truth, you felt nothing less than the nondual being and made a vital first step to enlightenment. If you didn't, don't worry, we will revisit the inner truth several times.

A fun fact about enlightenment is that you will never find it when looking for it. It has something to do with desire splitting your mind into subject and object, obscuring the nonduality— we will return to that. So, if you were taken off-guard and unexpectedly detected something in your mind, it is worth paying attention to it. You cannot find the nonduality by searching, but it is more likely to find *you* when you train your mind to notice it.

When you have learned where to look inside yourself, you can easily recognize your inner truth, that root sense of knowing, feeling, and perceiving. When you feel happy or sad, proud or ashamed, warm or cold, even without thinking *about* it, you always *know* you have these feelings. If you didn't know it, you wouldn't be conscious.

I can imagine a few objections to this statement. Many would argue that we aren't aware of most that goes on in our mind but that it influences our psyche all the same. Sigmund Freud (1856-1939) taught us about the workings of the *unconscious mind*. Past traumas can undeniably pose lots of challenges, even when someone is unaware of them. To dismiss this would be foolish.

The devil is again in the details. Is the unconscious mind part of consciousness or memory? To be conscious and unconscious of the same thing is irrational (a contradiction), so we have to conclude that the unconscious mind is memory only—until it interferes with the conscious mind and is not unconscious anymore. Simply said, if we want the word *knowing* to be meaningful, you cannot *be* happy or sad without *knowing* it, even when you probably don't continuously think *about* it.

To consider the unconscious mind part of the conscious mind is a typical dualistic misconception. We try to understand the makings and struggles of a third person's conscious mind. But have you ever met someone who experiences life from a third-person perspective? I don't think so. Third persons are imaginary: They don't exist! Everyone is a first person. Moreover, everyone is the *conscious experience* of a first person, and the unconscious mind is *not* part of that experience. We exist *exclusively* as conscious minds.

"Am I not my body then? For example, doesn't my hand exist? Isn't it part of my body and of me?" you might wonder. Of course, when you look at your exquisite hand, it seems real indeed. When it shakes a friend's hand, that friend's hand feels real as well, and it may seem ludicrous that it doesn't exist other than as first-person experience to both you and your friend.

But what you experience of your and your friend's hands, seeing them, feeling them, is mere present experience to both you and your friend. Does your hand exist independently of your conscious mind? It seems that it does because every morning when you wake up, you find it in its usual place at the end of your graceful arm, even though you weren't aware of it while you were sleeping. Its continuity suggests that it is real.

Yet, every aspect of your hand, its color, shape, feel, temperature, is sensory experience only. In the words of the eighteenth-century Scottish philosopher David Hume, your hand is a bundle of sensations. And what is left of your hand when there is no mind to perceive it? The typical dualistic assumption is that it is whatever a third person would experience. But since third persons don't exist, it is positively unknowable what your hand *is* when you are asleep, and no one else notices it either. Although counterintuitive, this is precisely David Hume's conclusion. Objects and body parts are bundles of sensations only and cannot be known to exist beyond that.

Back to your inner truth. We concluded that whatever you feel, including knowing something, is based on your inner truth. That inner truth is the essence of your consciousness. Not only does it "precede" all feelings, but it also "precedes" all perception: seeing, hearing, and so forth. What do *feeling* and *perception* have in common? They are instantaneous experiences, *present* experiences—happening *now*. Inner truth underlies *all* instantaneous experience.

Now we make a small step further. Did you ever experience anything in another moment than the present? Again, I don't think so. Maybe you remembered past experiences or imagined future experiences, but you always did so in the present. When you reminisce about a sunset last summer or dream about going skiing next winter, you do so *now*. All real, that is, not imagined experience, is *exclusively* present experience.

More and more, we are zeroing in on your inner truth. It "precedes" all feeling and perception, yet it is simultaneous because it is always *now*. It "underlies" the feeling of knowing something—knowing whether you're warm or cold, feel good or bad. Yet again, the inner truth is simultaneous, so it doesn't really "underly" feelings and perception but is an inseparable quality of them. Whenever you are conscious, it is there. Still, it always changes: Bad feelings turn into good ones, pain into relief, darkness into light, hate into love, and loathing into respect. What is the one thing that has been with you ever since you were a little kid? Ever since you can remember? What is it?

Our minds make us believe that what is permanent and immutable is real. Fleeting change slips through our fingers. We feel it is something we need to look past to find the unchanging reality. Our minds function this way, and Western thought is almost entirely built on that intuitive premise. Plato (c. 427-347 BCE), widely considered the godfather of Western thought, held that only the permanent "ideas" or "forms" abstracted from the perceived change could be considered real. In his Dialogues, Plato portrays philosopher Parmenides, who lived around 600 BCE, saying that the world is eternal and unchanging and that all change is an illusion.

Plato saw the physical world as an imitation of the eternal mathematical world. He revered mathematics. Whoever entered his Academy in Athens passed under a sign that said, "Let no one ignorant of geometry enter here." His trust in mathematics echoed Pythagoras (c. 570-495 BCE), who held that *all things are number* and that the cosmos comes from numerical principles.

Famously, the British philosopher Alfred North Whitehead (1861-1947) characterized all Western philosophy as "footnotes to Plato." Indeed, even the most extraordinary Western thinker of our era, Albert Einstein (1879-1955), believed that the equations of his brilliant theories were yet another step to discovering the "True Jacob," the "Secret of the Old One," so, the theory of everything and the mind-independent truth that is reality. In *Chapter 3*, we will review Einstein's views more thoroughly.

Mathematics has been instrumental in the world's progress—its power and relevance are beyond doubt. Mathematics is perfectly suited to analyze and understand the change patterns we experience. But does that mean that change is *not* real? Are our ultimate abstractions, the laws of nature that help us so accurately predict future change, real instead?

When you are driving a car at 65 mph (105 km/h), is there *anything* real about "65"? Or is your first-person experience of what it's like to drive a car at 65 mph real? I vote for the latter because what it's like to drive the car is instantaneous experience. The present driving experience before you even think *about* it leaves no time for doubt. In contrast, the number 65 means nothing if not interpreted in the experience of a conscious mind.

More than a century before Plato, before we came to see change as a distraction masking reality, Heraclitus (c. 535-475 BCE) saw it differently. He observed that the ever-present change is the essence of the world: "Everything flows." Who has the stronger case in your view? Plato or Heraclitus?

Again, my vote doesn't go to Plato. Experience favors Heraclitus: From a *real*, first-person viewpoint, *everything* in the present changes. Heraclitus put it this way: "No man can cross the same river twice." And there is *no* real change whatsoever in the past and future because they are imaginary. So, anything that doesn't change . . . isn't real! The persons and objects, forms and ideas that project permanence in your mind are imagined abstractions from present change only.

So, what is your inner truth? What is the essence of your conscious mind? What is the instantaneous root experience of feeling and perceiving before you can conceive, label, and store it in your memory? What is this ever-unique *now*? What is *existence*? You guessed it: *change*. *Change* is real. *Change* is your inner truth.

Change has always been with you ever since your earliest childhood memory. You have always been aware of it because it is your essence. It is impossible not to be conscious of change because the mere passing of time makes each moment unique—even when you usually don't think *about* change or pay attention to it. When there is consciousness, there is change; when there is change, there is consciousness.

And what if there is *no* consciousness? Is there still change? There *is* for third persons, but we already noticed they don't exist. So, we must admit that we are ignorant of *what is* when there is no consciousness. The rational conclusion is that change and consciousness are *identical* in terms of existence.

Many spiritual instructors teaching nondualism encourage us to look for something unmoving, eternal in our conscious experience. For example, Eckhart Tolle writes in *The Power of Now* that we can perceive "Being" through the gaps between our thoughts. He describes Being as an "abiding presence" and "unchanging deep stillness." Once you connect with it, says Tolle, you can bask in the eternal joy and peace it provides. I feel I get what he means. I was also fortunate to find the immense peace and joy of enlightenment.

But for me, and mere mortals like most of us, joy and tranquility don't always last. They still come and go. The key benefit of enlightenment is that you are on a profound level okay with that because you entirely accept your humanity, for better and for worse, including mood swings. If that is the inner peace that Tolle refers to, and I think, in a way, he does, then I fully agree with him.

As Heraclitus said, and as I suspect Tolle is perfectly aware of—he just uses different words—the only permanent "thing" is change. How does that work? Simple: What happens when change changes? It is still change! That is why change is permanent, without duration, without substance, without *opposite*, making each moment unique: the singular now. Change, which makes up the present and the conscious mind, is always there, even though it never stays the same.

What makes it so hard to grasp your inner truth of real, unconceived change (essential consciousness, the present, existence, instantaneous experience, . . .) is that when you want to talk or even think *about* it, you have to conceive it and commit it to your memory. You have to mentally glue a label on that memory and assign some words before sharing it with others. However, once conceived, real change isn't real change anymore. Once change is conceived, it is always imbued with some permanence. Real change cannot be conceived because, once conceived, change has become a *difference*.

For example, I can smell the spring blossom from the prune tree in our garden. In the singular present moment that I do so, this lovely experience remains unconceived and is nothing less than *change* itself. When I am in a poetic mood and want to sing my praises of spring blossom to my wife, I need to conceive the experience and possibly attribute some evocative metaphors to demonstrate the depths of my delicate soul—the soft violins of nature's overture and still fragile promise of spring.

I may hope to impress my wife with my blossom scent concepts—although I wouldn't count on it because she has a sensitive baloney radar—but my concepts aren't real blossom scent anymore. Like any instantaneous experience, real blossom scent is singular, so it doesn't have an opposite. And conceived blossom scent *does* have an opposite: simply *not* blossom scent.

All conceived change has its opposite in *not* that change. So, *anything* with an opposite is not real change; it is dual. Conceived change refers to a difference—a distinction, a contrast. *This* but not *that*. And both *this* and *that* have some permanence. *All* words refer to something permanent—otherwise, we couldn't use a word twice. They refer to concepts but not real change. So, whatever words refer to . . . doesn't exist! We cannot conceive immediate experience or communicate it. Ultimately, the change that is spring blossom scent, like all other instantaneous experience, must remain private.

Even though we cannot conceive immediate experience, all we ever talk *about* is *precisely* immediate experience. We cannot talk about anything else! Whatever we talk about are memories of immediate experience—possibly of other people's immediate experiences, and sometimes with extraordinarily high levels of abstraction. As long as we admit that we lack supernatural powers, everything that ever enters our memory—if it wasn't there already—must come from experience.

So, all unconceived experience is private knowledge, and all public knowledge is conceived experience. Since we are, by definition, conscious of our immediate experience, there is, in terms of existence, no difference between unconceived experience, unconceived knowledge, and unconceived change. Unconceived knowledge, just like all the other synonyms, is the same as your inner truth from the beginning of this chapter.

The present is change only. If your conscious mind weren't aware of it, there would be no reason to assume it existed. All change is mind-dependent because, without a mind, its existence is uncertain. This is why change is equal to the conscious mind. To consider that change can exist separately from the mind is not sustained by the facts and intrinsically dualistic.

The present change—that *is* your conscious mind—is singular. It precedes all distinctions: between right and wrong, warm and cold, sweet and salty, left and right. In the singular present, they are all undivided, *one*. Their split is the product of the conceiving mind, which commits and retrieves patterns of change as concepts (distinctions, contrasts, differences) to and from memory.

Your unconceived conscious experience itself is undoubtable because it is presently singular. It doesn't have an opposite and leaves no time for doubt. To deny that you have a conscious experience, you need a conscious experience, which means it is still there. In line with the undoubtable singularity of change, another synonym for the unconceived present experience is *truth*.

These are our preliminary conclusions:
- ✓ The unconceived experience that is the conscious mind *equals* change. Change equals existence. Existence cannot be doubted because in the present (that it is), there is no time to deny or doubt it. Hence, it is truth itself and precedes *all* distinctions. Unconceived experience equals unconceived knowledge from the immediate first-person perspective. Unconceived knowledge is exclusively private. Since it is undoubtable, unconceived knowledge is necessarily true.
- ✓ Conceived knowledge, consisting of *concepts*, is conceived experience. All concepts indicate distinctions. The differences concepts refer to do not *exist* because they are merely imagined *by* conscious minds *for* conscious minds. All knowledge that you ever read, hear, speak, or think *about* is conceived knowledge: knowledge that refers to non-existing differences. Concepts are never beyond doubt; they are never necessarily true.

In other words:
- ✓ The real conscious mind equals unconceived existence, which is in nothing different from unconceived knowledge, unconceived experience, and unconceived change. But *what* the conscious mind conceives is not real.
- ✓ Conceiving is real, but *what* it conceives is not.
- ✓ Knowing is real, but *what* it knows is not.
- ✓ Experiencing is real, but *what* it experiences is not.
- ✓ *How* life is, is real, but *what* life is, is not.

Where does that leave *reality* and our knowledge thereof?

Since we are an inseparable aspect of reality, we cannot know *what* reality is; we cannot know a world separate from the human mind. We only know what it's like to be an aspect of reality. Hence, we must conclude that what we conceive is *not* reality. Although nondualism doesn't deny reality's existence, it entails ignorance of reality—we cannot conceive mind-independent knowledge. We unduly objectify the subjective by claiming knowledge of reality.[4]

This is nondualistic metaphysics in a nutshell. We have arrived at it by factual, rational thinking about subjectivity. There is no cause for concern if you didn't follow it completely. We will explore it from different angles as well.

METAPHYSICS

I used the word *metaphysics* several times. But what is it? In contemporary dualistic empirical science, metaphysics has a bad reputation. Such science implicitly or explicitly assumes that physics should only study the *objective reality*, that is, simply *reality* or the *mind-independent truth*. It scorns metaphysics as subjective and scientifically meaningless. It holds that measurements and elegant mathematics can lead to empirically falsifiable statements, bringing humanity closer to understanding the "real world."

However, the assumption that mathematics, measurements, and testability are scientific is also metaphysical. The very fact that we are engaging in science is based on metaphysical beliefs. Metaphysics is about knowledge and truth; engaging in science demonstrates a belief in the value of truthful knowledge of the world.

---

[4] Even our *selves* are technically the product of unwarranted objectification. Yet, our universal fate of being unduly objectified is probably of little comfort to those who suffer from it.

What better way to understand what metaphysics actually is than the original treatise of Aristotle (384-322 BCE), which later became known as *Metaphysics*. Aristotle never used the word *metaphysics* but called it *the first philosophy*. He was aware that we cannot do science or other pursuits of knowledge without metaphysical assumptions. Aristotle put it as follows:

> ". . . if there were no other independent things besides the composite natural ones, the study of nature would be the primary kind of knowledge; but if there is some motionless independent thing, the knowledge of this precedes it and is first philosophy, and it is universal in just this way, because it is first. And it belongs to this sort of philosophy to study being as being, both what it is and what belongs to it just by virtue of being."

So, metaphysics is about understanding what exists and what we can know about existence. It seems so simple that even a 5-year-old can answer it. This green grass, that chair, my hands: their existence seems indisputable.

However, the greenness of grass needs to be perceived by a mind. Without a mind, there is merely electromagnetic radiation of a certain frequency (light), and when we are perfectly honest, we don't even know what that *is* in the absence of a mind. Does greenness exist separately from the mind? Can we have even the slightest idea of what is left of green grass without a mind? Does *anything* that we perceive and conceive exist separately from the mind? Is the world dual or nondual?

Metaphysics is hotly debated in philosophical circles. I make the case that the world is nondual. Duality is a powerful illusion. The greenness of grass does *not* exist without a mind, and for the same reason, *nor does anything else*. There is mind only, and it comprises *everything*. *That* is nondualism. Anything less cannot be truly considered nondualism.

Many believe in evolution and a material explanation of the

mind. Others have had spiritual experiences and felt contact with the nonduality. But as long as they also believe that, for example, the Grand Canyon exists separately from the mind, they are still implicitly dualistic—because the mind and the rest of the world are not one. We could call them *monistic dualists*. Before I experienced satori, I was one of them.

How about you? Do you believe the bed you sleep in still exists when you are in a dreamless sleep? If you do, then you are also still a dualist. A nondualist must conclude that the bed cannot be known to exist beyond awareness of it. Like any other object, the bed is a non-existing entity that the mind imagines to predict and steer present experience.

Nondualistic metaphysical insight is still rare. The culprit is not complexity but seeming implausibility: It fundamentally contradicts our deepest intuitions. But intuitions aren't always accurate.

Those about to give up on this book may remind themselves that things aren't always what they seem. The earth isn't flat. In a vacuum, heavy objects don't fall faster than light ones. A car that accelerates to twice its speed has increased its energy not twofold but fourfold. Time and space are not separate phenomena but a single one called spacetime. Centrifugal forces and gravity seem different phenomena as well but are also just one: Einstein's *bending* of spacetime. We cannot reach the end of a rainbow. And reality... is not accessible to the human mind. The conclusion is logically inevitable if we refrain from supernatural speculation.

Not only scientists but also spiritual seekers can be dualistic. The implicit or explicit belief in a mind-independent truth is behind the split that both dualistic scientists *and* dualistic spiritual seekers habitually envision: In their view, science is about the objective reality and spirituality about subjective experience. It is fairly common for spiritual seekers to consider science and rational thought matters from a different planet than their spiritual practice, hostile to the openness required

2. AWAKENING AND THE RESULTING MINDSET

for a holistic experience. At best, dualistic scientists and spiritual dualists respectfully refuse to thread on each other's territories.

Now I must make another bold statement that may cause objections. Yet it is, both rationally speaking and in my conviction, undoubtedly so: A spiritual seeker who understands the subjective world of spiritual practice as separate from the physical realms of science and rational thought is *not* enlightened.

The spiritual seeker may have had the most astounding spiritual experiences and be touched by the nonduality. However, the belief in a separation between the physical and mental world is still highly dualistic. The impression that spirituality and science are incompatible is a symptom of the same dualistic illusion that enlightened teachers want you to become aware of.

Spiritual practice can lead to enlightenment and deep nondualistic insight. But when it does, it must include the physical world as well. Nondualistic metaphysics is the link between spirituality on the one hand and reason and science on the other—as illustrated in *Figure 1*.

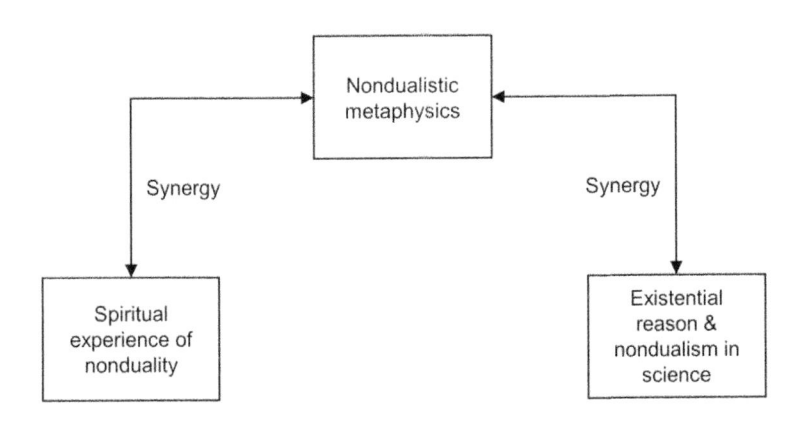

Figure 1 Nondualistic metaphysics, spirituality, reason, and science

Nondualistic metaphysics and spiritual experience mutually deepen nondualistic awareness. The two-way arrow indicates their synergetic relationship. Since it is the first philosophy, accurate metaphysics is also a prerequisite for nondualism in science and other rational thought.

In *Existential Rationalism,* I explain how dualism impairs contemporary science. The irrational belief in our ability to conceive mind-independent knowledge engenders further irrationality. However, the book you are reading now is not about science. We will investigate existential reason, though, which is reason compatible with the fact that our subjectivity is inescapable. Nondualistic metaphysics and existential reason are also a two-way street—one we will explore extensively.

Nondualism is a thoroughly interconnected subject. To explain it in more detail, I need to choose a starting point. I prefer to stay close to myself and use reason: The unyielding world forces engineers like me to be rational and practical, and avoid unwarranted flights of the imagination.[5]

Reason aims at reducing confusion by remaining factual about how the natural world behaves—without supernatural storytelling, without trying to explain the inexplicable. Magical and super-human experiences are fascinating but not natural: They aren't understandable to the human mind. More than anything, reason is about increasing clarity by being meaningful, unequivocal, and consistent in the choice of words.

So, for a rational approach to nondualism, we must select our words diligently. Spiritual seekers and rational thinkers need to speak the same language. Words aren't merely pointers to a spiritual experience but also the potential catalysts for integrating nondualism into science and Western philosophy.

I noticed that spiritual teachers often give words a second,

---

[5] Some lesser-informed souls may feel that our lack of imagination makes us engineers dull. We may not always be the life of the party, but imagine how dull your life would be without us! No internet, no social media, and no planes to bring you to Rome or Paris.

spiritual meaning. Sometimes, they capitalize words to distinguish between their common and special spiritual meaning. We already saw Eckhart Tolle using the word *Being* to indicate the nondual existence. In his model of enlightenment, the *mind* gets in the way of contact with *Being*. For Tolle, the mind is not the conscious mind but merely the thinking mind. According to Tolle, we are *unconscious* as long as we think because we aren't in touch with *Being*. To become *conscious*, we need to stop thinking so that we leave our *egoic mind* behind and get in contact with nondual *Being*.

Tolle is well aware that concepts can't convey an awakening experience, so he cautions us not to get hung up on his words. His vocabulary points to the nonduality but can be forgotten once contact is established. His words are powerful, truthful, and inspiring. But their special meaning creates confusion outside of spirituality. For example, it will be hard to convince all psychologists to no longer consider thinking a conscious activity. And most people have an idea of what their *self* points at (themselves), but what is the difference with *ego*? Is it just the self but only for whatever has a negative connotation?

Inadvertently, Tolle does what is common in so many areas of human activity: create jargon that distinguishes insiders and keeps out outsiders. In order to bridge the dualistic divide, we cannot afford the luxury of creating islands of meaning, blissfully disconnected from other realms. Our choice of words should be coherent. To give normal words a special second spiritual meaning is renouncing the dream of widespread nondualistic understanding. Tolle strongly advocates more nondualistic awareness in the world. So do I. We could reach more people by bridging the divide between spiritual and rational nonduality. Instead of using special words for special experiences, I suggest rediscovering the special meaning of common words.

The Enlightenment Experience

Your inner truth of *knowing*, which is identical to immediate experience, is undeniable. But *what* it knows—concepts—can be quite inaccurate. Without going too deep into the philosophy of truth, we have learned from the seventeenth-century rationalist René Descartes that what the mind thinks is never beyond doubt. The only certainty it has is that it thinks. In his 1641 *Meditations*, Descartes defines *thought* as "what happens in me such that I am immediately conscious of it, insofar as I am conscious of it." So, his *thought* is more than just cognition: It is the inner truth of knowing that precedes the split between truthfulness and falsehood. Descartes accurately observes that we can't deny this inner truth.

Yet, we cannot communicate the certainty of inner truth to others. In communication, we are limited to sending and receiving concepts—verbally or not. So, whoever will explain the enlightenment experience to you has to do so conceptually—even when coaching you in spiritual practice and focusing on feelings.

Some who have achieved enlightenment via spiritual experience, like Eckhart Tolle, maintain that thinking is an obstacle to enlightenment. He suggests we should "switch off" our thinking to become nondually aware through the empty "spaces" between our thoughts. Although I got my nondualistic awareness through metaphysical insight and cannot get it a second time, so I cannot verify it, I am convinced that Tolle's approach works.

However, enlightenment by metaphysical insight does *not* require deliberately stopping to think. Instead, it suggests using rational thought to deepen your metaphysical understanding. Once sufficient clarity is achieved, the nondualistic awareness no longer finds any obstacles in irrational beliefs and can come "rolling into" the primed and receptive mind. Although prepared by "mundane" reason, that experience of suddenly and instantly passing through a wormhole from the conceptual world where you thought you resided into the present that encompasses the whole universe is . . . simply overwhelming.

※

When we have an overwhelming experience, we often say it is beyond words. But did you realize that *all* experiences are ultimately beyond words? For example, we all know the difference between warm and cold. But if we have to put into words what distinguishes them, we can only repeat . . . one is warm and the other cold. We will never know what warm and cold are like for someone other than ourselves, even though we seem to have remarkably similar experiences.

Once we put a subjective, instantaneous experience into words, those words are merely empty labels, meaningless until they trigger an instantaneous experience in a receiver's mind—from memory. We cannot know if such subjective experience is the same between individuals because instantaneous experience remains private.

Can experience be *not* subjective or *not* instantaneous? No! All experience needs a subject, and experience that is not instantaneous is merely *imagined* from memory by a subject in the immediate present. All experience you ever remember or imagine, you remember and imagine *now*. This means that *all* experience is private. The enlightenment experience is no exception to this rule.

To explain an experience to someone, we have to point to something in the hope that the other person recognizes our experience in themselves: "Do you like the color of this rose?" Often, enlightenment is presented as such a special experience that we can only give pointers to explain it. While this is entirely true, it is revealing that this is also the case for *all* other experiences.

So, all subjective experience is ultimately beyond words, and enlightenment is no exception. But just like with any other experience, if we want to talk about it anyway, we have to use words all the same. I'd call enlightenment an epiphany that revolutionizes your mind. It radically changes the way you see . . . everything.

Before the epiphany, you take it for granted that your mind holds an image of the real world surrounding you. You feel you can use your mind to predict what will happen in that real world, for example, by checking the weather forecast. At night, your mind goes to sleep while the "real world" keeps on turning. The next morning, your mind checks in again on the real world. Was the weather forecast accurate?

During the epiphany, you suddenly become aware that the image in your mind is not the real world at all but that only your mind itself is real. So, what *is* the real world when you are sleeping? That is forever beyond us! And why can we nonetheless forecast the weather? Because we may not conceptually understand our existence, but that doesn't mean we are incompetent or unintelligent.

The images of the real world you formerly took for reality reveal themselves as mere figments of the imagination because they conceive something separate from the mind. It becomes clear that the images your mind conjures up have no meaning beyond that mind and that they only serve to predict and steer your experience. *Multiplicity* is an illusion; there aren't multiple beings, creatures, *things*, but just undivided being. This realization is known as *satori*.

You suddenly see the conscious mind before it conceives anything for *what*, no, better, for *how* it is: not separate from *everything*, and since it is not separate, it is not so much *part of* all there is but indeed all there is. The words *part of* imply a subdivision, but the present conscious experience isn't subdivided. It is singular. The realization of the conscious experience's full extent, this deep-felt oneness with all existence, is the natural step after satori and can be called *finding Tao*. Tao is nondual existence.

2. AWAKENING AND THE RESULTING MINDSET

For thousands of years, the word *Tao* has been used to indicate the nonduality, the nondual existence that *is* the mind—particularly in the East. Accordingly, I prefer to use the word *Tao* instead of Tolle's *Being*.

Tao is what you and I are, but many people are unaware of their Tao essence—hence the words *finding* Tao for the second enlightenment step. In my personal experience, finding Tao followed satori a few minutes later. The total enlightenment experience from satori to finding Tao probably lasted less than ten minutes (I didn't check my watch). The amazement at it is much more enduring. When I write this, my awe before the nonduality already lasts seven years and doesn't wane at all. For example, it impels me to write. Tao is an endless source of marvel one can easily spend a lifetime contemplating.

The Copernican metaphysical perspective reversal of enlightenment is illustrated in *Figure 2*. The upper image is the classical pre-enlightenment dualistic understanding of the world. We detect an outside reality via our senses, and our brain forms an image of that outside reality in our mind. The separation between reality and the mind is what makes this worldview dualistic.

Below, the second image shows the metaphysical aspect of satori. Satori is the first enlightenment step. It is the realization that the separate world we conceive doesn't have mind-independent existence. We understand that the outside world, the inside world of our body, and the *self* are imagined by the mind only and cannot be known to exist beyond their imagination.

The bottom image shows the metaphysical aspect of the second enlightenment step: finding Tao. The mind now fully grasps nondualistic metaphysics. It no longer understands itself as separate from the outside and inside world but as one with them. When enlightened people see a tree, they are convinced that, in terms of existence, the tree is as much an aspect of themselves as their senses, brain, and the rest of their body.

Existence is appreciated as Tao: *identical* to the conscious mind, to the present, to unconceived knowledge, experience, and *change*. Tao is found when existence and all its synonyms are fathomed as the nonduality. In the third image, the mind is represented as a dashed cloud. The dashes indicate that the mind is not limited: What is outside the cloud is mind too. In a nondual world, everything is mind.

2. AWAKENING AND THE RESULTING MINDSET

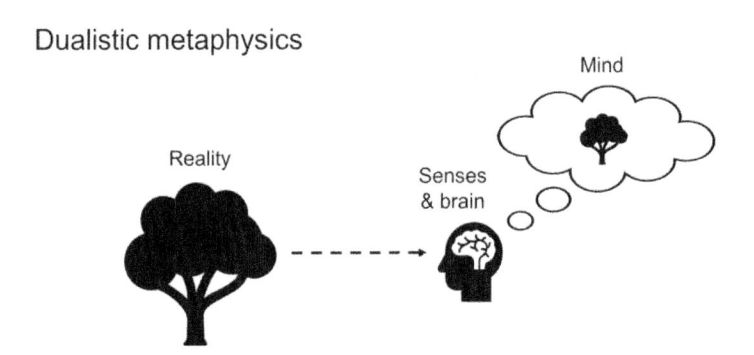

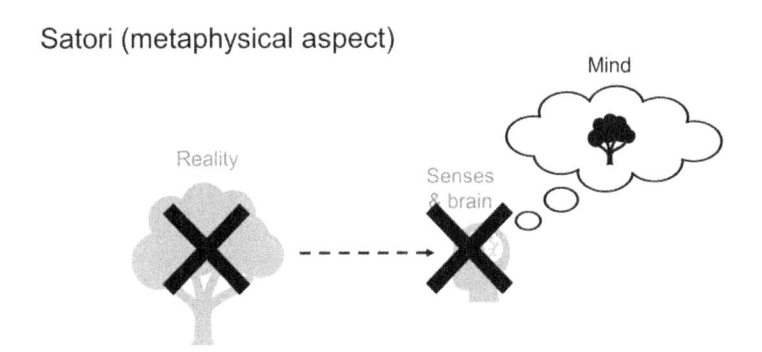

Dualistic metaphysics

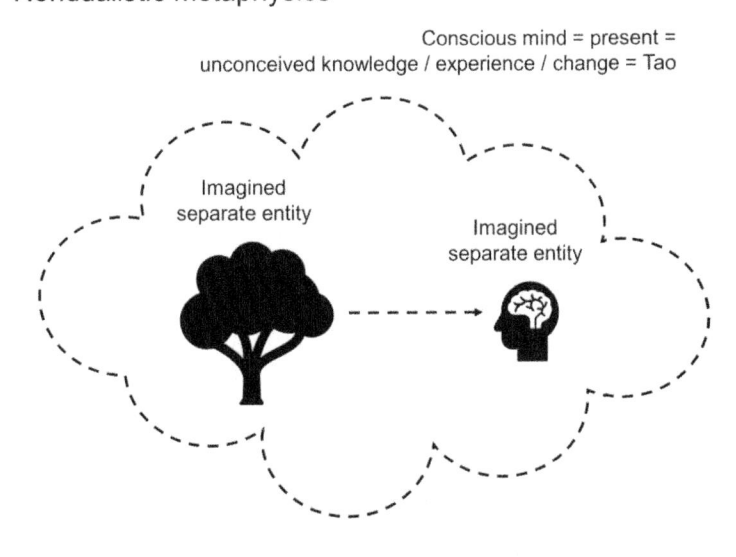

Satori (metaphysical aspect)

Nondualistic metaphysics

Conscious mind = present =
unconceived knowledge / experience / change = Tao

Figure 2 Nondualistic metaphysics

Those interested in philosophy may reckon that nondualistic metaphysics looks awfully similar to George Berkeley's *subjective idealism*. However, there are fundamental differences. Berkeley (1685-1753) was an Anglo-Irish philosopher. His subjective idealism states that "to be is to be perceived." Objects exist as "ideas" only, perceived by "spirits." Spirits are different from ideas in that they cannot be perceived. In this constellation, it is unclear why two people perceive the same world, albeit from different perspectives. Berkeley solves this by positing that the unperceived world still exists because God perceives it.

Berkeley is nowadays considered a subjective monist because he denies the existence of a mind-independent material world. Berkeley's world exists solely of spirits and ideas, so as pure subjectivity.[6]

In contrast, nondualism states that the perceived distinction between spirit (subject) and idea (object) is an illusion. Nondualism understands the mind as the inseparable combination of subject and object at once. So, different people perceive the same world because they partake in the same subject-object combination: Tao. Hence the mind cloud's dashed line in the bottom figure. Berkeley's "monistic" subjective idealism would be better represented by a solid line instead because his "ideas" are reality.

Enlightenment is an epiphany, a flash of insight, an *Aha!* moment. But that is not the whole story. Tao's riddle is different from other riddles. When I ask which month has 28 days, you might have an *Aha!* moment because your mind

---

[6] Although Berkeley denies the existence of a mind-independent world, he doesn't deny the separate existence of ideas and spirits. Accordingly, subjective idealism would be better described as a monistic dualism than a monism.

2. AWAKENING AND THE RESULTING MINDSET

knows the answer.[7] However, when you find Tao, your mind *is* the answer: Conceived existence coincides with unconceived existence.

Suddenly, clear as day, you discover Tao in your conscious experience: your deepest yet completely available essence. Tao is more than metaphysical. It is spiritual. You not only find the solution to a specific puzzle, as Archimedes did sitting in the bathtub having his *Eureka!* moment, but you solve nothing less than the entire puzzle of existence—by simply seeing past it. *All* existential questions are at once sufficiently answered because Tao is the answer before any question can crystallize.

- ✓ What is my purpose in life? Tao!
- ✓ How should I live? Tao!
- ✓ What is my free will? Tao!
- ✓ Who am I, and why do I experience life as I do? Tao!

Tao is not a separate mystical presence but the inner truth of being that always accompanies you. There is no existential answer required beyond Tao because the more you inquire and cogitate, the further you move away from the all-encompassing truth that you already are.

For example, those still dualistically inclined may want to understand what causes the instantaneous, private, subjective experience known as Tao. The conviction that third persons are real gives contemporary Western dualistic philosophers reason to believe that some experience is *not* subjective and instantaneous.

Round and round they go, chasing their tails by using their experience to explain their experience—which needs no explanation because it is already entirely known. While doing so, they fail to notice that the only way to grasp their experience entirely is to stop conceptualizing and pay attention to their essence: Tao.

Once you have found Tao, existential guidance comes

---

[7] Every month.

naturally:
- ✓ What should I do? Whatever I do is okay.
- ✓ What should I think? Whatever I think is fine.
- ✓ Which decision should I take? The one you feel you should take. The one in Tao, even when Tao tells you to investigate, ponder, or doubt a little longer.
- ✓ How should I be? Precisely as I am because nothing is missing in Tao. I am already whole.

Finding Tao makes you instantly congruent with your being. You no longer see yourself as separate from your objectives. You no longer seek to find yourself or live according to rules that split your being into how you are versus how you ought to be. Instead, you discover that it is impossible to live inauthentically when you incorporate Tao's instantaneous directions. Your attention's center of gravity is shifted for good: from the conceptual worlds of the past and future to the inconceivable now.

The enlightenment experience is often preceded by a conundrum that cannot be solved conceptually. Eckhart Tolle describes his existential crisis before his awakening, and I suffered one or two of sorts as well, albeit not as severe as Tolle's. In Zen-Buddhist monasteries, teachers use koans—seemingly absurd or paradoxical little stories, statements, or questions—to confuse their students, nudging their attention away from analysis and thought to the immediate experience.

When we have bumped our head sufficiently often on a closed door and have become aware of the limitations of thought, we can start looking elsewhere for answers and may find Tao. In my case, enlightenment passed through metaphysical insight, but my openness flowed from pure emotion. The conceptual worlds I had built in my mind had become nightmarish. I needed a way out so badly that my mind was ready to receive nondualistic insight.

Once I did find Tao, the weight of my problems fell off my shoulders. A deep peace overcame me. I felt I had come home and found everything I had ever been looking for. Nothing was missing anymore in my life. I was complete. That inner peace has never left me since and is always available for me to tap into. Even when I am still impatient at times, on a deeper level, I remain at peace.

An intriguing moment during enlightenment is the precise moment one fathoms the nonduality. Before, the world is neatly subdivided into mind and reality. Whenever the dualistic mind wants to get to the bottom of reality, it stumbles upon infinite regressions. For example, when we want to know the cause of our existence, we can, like a child, forever ask, "Why?" one more time until we don't know how to answer anymore. Individual life - human life - genetic material - evolution - extinction of dinosaurs - primordial soup - big bang - . . . ?

Similarly, Cartesian dualism implies that our physical brain holds a witness to the world image projected into it. But does that mean that this inner witness also has a brain, which, in turn, houses another witness? And so on.

Once you fathom the nonduality, your "reality concepts" suddenly collapse into the present. The present reveals itself as the universe's enigma you are an aspect of. Once you see past the illusory nature of the self, other people and creatures, and the physical world, you're bound to give up on all conceptual certainties. The leap into the present takes courage because you must let go of everything you thought you could hold on to.

But once you take that leap into the present, the illusion of your separation from everyone and everything is gone, and suddenly . . . there is no endless regression anymore. Instead of going around in circles by looking for conceptual answers to explain your experience, you understand that whatever you conceive is further away from your essential truth of unconceived experience.

The infinity you were projecting outside of yourself in the form of endless regressions reveals itself as your infinite being. Your presence is no longer limited by space, time, or form. Tao has no boundaries because it is unconceived. It is consciousness. It is change. It is present. It is existence. It is truth. To mentally merge with the Tao that you are is an endless plunge. Suddenly, your life's seemingly infinite separate facets line up, and you see the big undivided picture of your existence. Endless looping is no longer required because you have become one with your limitless being.

After fathoming Tao, you look around and say, "Look, there's a tree. That's me. And there's another person. That's me as well." You see the sky, the landscape, the sun, and the stars, and you know that they are in nothing different from your being. They are, like you, one with boundless being. And since that being is boundless, it is not just one. It is also definitely not two. It is uncountable. Hence, we call it *nondualism* instead of *monism*.

Since you have come this far in the book without tossing it aside in disbelief, perhaps you think, "This enlightenment business sounds good! Where can I get myself some?" But I must caution that the nonduality cannot be seized intellectually. Fathoming Tao, making the endless plunge into the mystery that you are, is a spontaneous experience you cannot "take." Enlightenment has to be given to you because you will never find it as long as you search—or even *hope* for it. Searching and hoping split your mind into a subject and an object. You cannot be aware of Tao's subject-object unity as long as you do that.

Some prepare for enlightenment through spiritual practice. Meditation has led people to enlightenment for thousands of years. However, I know far too little about that path to comment on it.

In order to prepare the mind for enlightenment via metaphysical insight, seekers may correct irrational beliefs that obstruct nondualistic clarity. A compelling way of doing so is by prompting introspection with some questions: "When I close my eyes, how do I know that I am still aware and not sleeping? Where does that feeling of being aware come from?

What does my consciousness consist of? What does it feel like? How does it relate to the outside world?"

The more consistent your answers are, the less resistance enlightenment will encounter when it finds you.

THE ENLIGHTENED MINDSET

When you conceive the change that is Tao, the resulting conceived Tao is no longer change but has become a *difference* since it contrasts with its opposite, *not* Tao. Your memory of Tao, which is conceived knowledge, is not the same as the unconceived Tao. So, when you are enlightened and have found Tao, Tao itself remains *cognitively* a mystery even to yourself, notwithstanding your full knowledge of it in its unconceived "state."

What makes the mind enlightened is that it has discovered its unconceived essence. Hence, Tao's boundless, sublime simplicity is private and cannot be conveyed. In the sixth century BCE, Lao Tzu put it as follows in his *Tao Te Ching*: "The Tao that can be told is not the true Tao."

Accordingly, *you* are the expert on your spiritual awakening. Talking about it with others can be remarkably useful, but, as with all instantaneous experience, only you know what it's like—to you. And since the experience involves dispelling the illusion of self, somehow, enlightenment invites humility rather than boastfulness.

But you also don't *need* confirmation of your awakening because the perspective reversal is so drastic and unmistakable that you will be certain of your Tao discovery. If you still have doubts, you may have glimpsed the nonduality but haven't yet found Tao.

Experientially, nondualistic metaphysics makes perfect sense to the enlightened mind. However, cognitively, the mind never entirely stops protesting such counterintuitive notions as the inexistence of *differences* like the self and the physical world. In terms of evolution, the thinking mind is *made* to perceive differences and to take these differences seriously. Considering that you should—or even could—entirely stop thinking after a spiritual awakening is a fallacy and illusion. The powerful benefit of enlightenment is that it corrects your *beliefs* about the nature of the differences you conceive. You see them for what they are: not real, but more often than not entirely relevant to your life.

As a human being, you think up differences, including your entire life. Life has a certain duration and an opposite in *not* life (or death). Consequently, life is conceptual and not identical to Tao's unconceived existence. However, it isn't necessary or recommended to renounce your life. Tao is not about nihilism—at all.

Once you have found Tao, you can *quiet* your thinking and listen to what Tao tells you. This is an easy way to learn what you want deep inside your heart. I cannot look inside your heart, but I am pretty sure that most people will find in Tao, inside their nondual hearts, that there *are* loved ones, other people and creatures, likes and dislikes, and things that matter in their lives, even though they don't exist beyond the mind's imagination.

Existence, Tao, is *change*, but life is *differences*. We exist in the "change world" but live in the "differences world"—also known as *samsara*, as we will discuss later. Nonduality involves renouncing an escape from your human mind and making peace with it instead, precisely as it is. As long as you don't fully accept that you imagine concepts that matter to you—while realizing that they don't exist separately from your mind—you won't have such peace.

Some spiritual seekers seem convinced that nondualistic awareness is about feeling only and has nothing to do with thinking. They might argue that we should learn "to trust our feelings again" and perhaps suggest that we have lost the ability to do so because of "conditioning by society." But precisely which feeling should we trust? Once more, the devil is in the details.

What could be your mental attitude toward thinking after enlightenment? What changes? The nondualistic awareness resulting from enlightenment is a perspective reversal—your attention default shifts from the imagined worlds of concepts to the unconceived present. In terms of existence, nothing changes, but psychologically, *everything* does. You no longer consider yourself separate from what you conceive and perceive because everything is *the present* only.

Enlightenment removes an illusion and provides you with unfettered access to the nonduality that you entirely know yet cannot and *need not* conceive or cognitively understand. Discerning your pre-conceptual existence liberates you from the confusing mirages that distract you from the *now*. You free up mental energy for what matters most.

So, what feeling should we learn to trust? This feeling is *not* the opposite of thinking; it isn't separate from that. The feeling you're looking for is identical to Tao, doesn't have an opposite, and is inseparable from everything that's going on in your mind, including your thinking.

What you think *about* are concepts: imagined, hypothetical experiences. But thinking *itself* is a real present experience. So Tao is still available when you're thinking. Once you see past the illusion of conceptual reality, you can even connect with the present *during* thought.

While it can be tremendously helpful to retreat into calm solitude to meditate and introspect on the way to enlightenment, once you *are* enlightened, you don't have to concentrate and tell yourself to stop thinking anymore. You don't have to close your eyes and block all other sensory inputs to be in touch with your nondual existence. Tao is omnipresent, whether or not you think, look, listen, touch, or talk. Accessing Tao is not about decreeing yourself to stop doing things, because mental rules split your mind.

Instead, to be in touch with the nonduality, you merely have to turn your attention to the present, to your unconceived experience, before your thinking mind tries to *hold on* to it. You can access it while meditating, grocery shopping, playing golf, or talking with friends. Tao is the feeling of *being*, which is in nothing different from *what it's like to be. That* is the feeling you are looking for. You can recognize Tao always and anywhere after its discovery. It can always provide peace and the sincerest advice.

Mindfulness and meditation coaches frequently point to the conscious mind's *witnessing presence*. Through meditation, you can rest your conscious experience in this witnessing presence and put yourself, as an observer, at a distance from the concepts and feelings arising in your mind. This practice did wonders for me to feel peaceful and calm.

However, we should distinguish the witnessing presence from Tao. Tao includes your witnessing presence *and* feelings and musing insofar as they are unconceived experience. If you identify too much with your witnessing presence, you dualistically partition your mind.

After leaving your meditation den, you will also notice that keeping up a witnessing presence and managing your daily chores simultaneously is challenging. Neuroscientists have established that your mind's short-term memory can only hold a handful of items. If you constantly have to center on a witnessing presence, it will be hard to remain truly open to the present.

Nondualistic awareness allows you to maintain contact with Tao without paying attention. How does that work? Let me use an analogy: When you are on a beach, and the sun sets over the water, you probably aren't worried that the sun will make the sea boil over or that the sea will extinguish the sun. Your beliefs are rational and accurate: The earth isn't flat, and the sun doesn't move around the earth.

Similarly, the best means of staying in touch with the nondual present is clarity about your existence, rooted in reason and experience. Once achieved, drawing on the limitless Tao becomes second nature and requires no attention at all.

※

A crucial aspect of nonduality is the nature of free will. It is easier to trust Tao when you have compatible beliefs about free will. I can best explain the nondualistic take on free will by contrasting it to Sam Harris's position. In 2012, he published a book about it, aptly named *Free Will*. Harris is a monistic dualist: His nondualism in spiritual matters collides with dualism in scientific and philosophical matters.

In his book, Harris argues that free will is an illusion. Harris understands the physical world to be deterministic, and since the physical brain produces the mind, the mind must also be predetermined.[8] Harris's dualism is revealed by his view that the physical brain causes the mind: a highly intuitive but not entirely rational premise.

If the brain is material and the mind immaterial, a supernatural interface must exist between the material and immaterial world. Supernatural suppositions are irrational because they explain with the inexplicable. In other words, they aren't explanations at all. There is undeniably a strong correlation between brain areas and the conscious experience, but that doesn't substantiate an objective causal relation between them because the entire brain cannot be known to exist separately from the immaterial mind.

The conscious experience cannot be pinpointed at all, so also not in the physical brain. René Descartes already noticed

---

[8] Following the same material explanation of the mind, Western philosophers from Thomas Hobbes (1558-1669) to Daniel Dennet (born 1942) conclude that consciousness itself must be an illusion. They adhere to physical, *"objective"* monism, in contrast to Berkeley's *subjective* monism. Doubting the existence of consciousness is an elegant solution to the mind-matter interaction problem. But how do they explain that they doubt their consciousness? A home run for Descartes!

in his 1641 *Meditations* that surmising the location of the conscious experience anywhere in the body is incorrect. He used the example of *phantom pain* to demonstrate that the whereabouts of conscious experiences are imagined by the mind. Neuroscientists who look for the magical brain process that makes us experience, for example, blue as we do, are chasing their tails. The physical world doesn't cause our existence; it is merely an abstraction of it.[9]

Harris explains that we perceive freedom in our choices because we lack awareness of all the factors that determine our thoughts and actions. Although Harris considers free will a trick played by the mind on its owner, he considers it a healthy illusion. He argues we'd best cognitively accept that it is an illusion yet be swayed by it to have the pleasant feeling that we are free and our choices matter. So, Harris invites us to put faith in self-deception, which violates the rational principle of non-contradiction.

Perhaps the most convincing argument against seeing free will as an illusion is that it's inconceivable that evolution would have endowed us with such a fancy mind trick. What would be the biological value of it? Automatic behavior is far more efficient and swift than conscious behavior. So, free will as an illusion violates a second rational principle: sufficient reason. In total, there are four such principles of rational thought. We find them back in the next chapter.

What is the nondualistic understanding of free will? It starts with nondualistic metaphysics: Substance doesn't create the mind, but the mind creates substance. The physical brain doesn't create consciousness, but consciousness imagines the physical brain—as it imagines all other concepts.

So, nondualism agrees with Harris that the free will *concept*

---

[9] Another argument against the material brain causing the immaterial mind is as follows: *Material* and *medium* are etymological cousins, sharing their origin in the *mother* concept. The *material* brain "mothering" the *immediate*—"mother-less"— mind phenomena is a contradiction in terms.

is an illusion. All concepts refer to illusory entities, and free will is no exception. However, *unconceived* free will is *not* an illusion. Harris dualistically sees free will as a property of the mind. Instead, nonduality implies that free will, the conscious *agency* experience, is not separable from the total conscious experience. Since free will is an essence—what you *are*—it cannot be an illusion. You are not a subject at a distance from an objective reality but both subject and object simultaneously. So, your active experience of free will is as real as it gets.

Since Harris sees the mind as the product of the physical brain, he concludes, "Free will [...] cannot be made conceptually coherent. Either our wills are determined by prior causes and we are not responsible for them, or they are the product of chance and we are not responsible for them." Indeed, Harris's dualism contradicts moral responsibility.[10] But once we appreciate that our minds and free wills are not separate from the world, we must rationally conclude that people aren't only observers and victims. We are *agents* as well.

In Harris's objective world, we must discover our fate by observing it. In a nondual world, we instead discover our fate by creating it. Nondualism profoundly changes your beliefs and attitudes in life. That is why it is so important to get it right.

But if free will is real (in its unconceived "state"), doesn't that make us responsible for everything that goes wrong in our lives? Isn't free will too heavy a burden to bear? Doesn't it condemn us to the paranoid existence of a constant battle with adversity in which we can only trust ourselves?

Not to those who turn to Tao for guidance.

Our organism, with its ancestors and predecessors, has a billions-of-years-long track record of solving our problems for us. The Tao of our conscious experience is an expression of that. So, we don't have to take all the world's suffering on our

---

[10] There are no consistent arguments against fatalism if free will is considered an illusion. Secular dualism thus invites apathy and negligence.

shoulders and feel crushed by the enormity of our responsibility. Tao can always give counsel and solace. How does Tao do that?

Tao is sovereign because it is the undoubtable given of the present. If there is but one thing certain in life (besides death and taxes, I imagine you thinking), it is the spontaneous conscious experience accompanying you in the now. So, if you look for a harbor to find shelter, you need no lucky charm, mantra, mental anchor, or breathing exercise. You merely need to open up to the present in all its majestic simplicity to find everything you need.

Your present being will always tell you what to do because it does it for you, even when you don't think about it. Of course, you can also choose *not* to trust your being. But what does that bring? Not to trust the mind, world, and body you were born into? You still need that mind, world, and body. So, the reasonable choice is to trust your being. It frees up mind space. Still, when you let Tao guide you, you must be conscientious and cautious sometimes. But Tao will also let you know when.

Epicurus meets Einstein

"Greetings! I am Epicurus. With whom do I have the pleasure?"

"Albert Einstein, nice to meet you, Epicurus."

"Nice to meet you too, Albert. My compliments on your hairstyle! I knew the barbaric look would catch on. Casual cool, effortless chic."

"It's relatively simple, Epicurus; I have more important things on my mind than haircuts. And in the morning, I don't have time to comb my hair because I need to write down the equations I dream up when I sleep."

"Interesting frame of reference; I will mention it to my stylist slave Gaston the next time I see him. He adores hearing about tomorrow's trends! But let's talk philosophy now, Albert. The author told me you and

I have a lot in common."

"We do, Epicurus. We are both champions of reason and science, sworn enemies of superstition, but don't deny God's existence."

"That's right. Even when science explains all the phenomena in the world, the immediate arising of the phenomena in the conscious mind itself must remain a mystery because any explanation must also arise as a phenomenon in the conscious mind. So, the human mind has to deal with an inherent mystery, and I don't know enough about religion to claim that God isn't a proper way of dealing with that mystery for those who choose to do so. Besides, the gods have inspired us to organize some fabulous religious festivals. You should come and join me! On the twentieth of each month, we give ourselves to pleasure, wine, music, and dance to honor the gods."

"I appreciate your invitation but must decline because you are beyond my event horizon."

"No problem. Just maybe, the next time you savor a sip of wine, you could think of me. My name has survived the eons because it lives on in the minds of those whose only sin is the love of the good life."

"I promise I'll do that."

"Much appreciated! And as far as the gods are concerned, my only point is that we should not fear them. I believe philosophy serves a purpose: the well-being of people. And we can use philosophy and reason to conclude that the gods cannot harm us since they are independent of human existence and have no business in influencing it. Are you religious, Albert?"

"As a matter of fact, I am."

"What do you believe?"

"I believe in truth independent of the mind. I know its existence cannot be empirically verified, so it is my religion, a faith-based assumption. In my view, science is not possible without that assumption. That is why I believe it. Take the moon, for example: Do you believe it disappears when we don't look at it? When it is not 'in our minds'? If you believe the moon is still there when you don't look at it, you believe in truth independent of the mind. Just like me."

"I'm not going to argue with you on that one. I will meet Lao Tzu in the next chapter. The author told me he has something to say about it. I

will ask him."

"Thank you, Epicurus. While we are on faith-based assumptions, I understand that you believe the mind to be a mechanism of bouncing atoms. But how does consciousness arise from such a mechanical process? How can we have free will if the atom's movements are predetermined?"

"Look, Albert, the atoms aren't merely bouncing around; they are swerving: *moving in predictable patterns but with an added touch of randomness. This randomness explains why we cannot completely predict the world and have free will."*

"And why do they swerve?"

"Such is nature."

"Oh my, you sound just like Sam Harris, a popular thinker you will also meet. Harris uses the perceived randomness of quantum objects to explain that we aren't entirely responsible for our behavior, even though he considers the mind preordained. He sees us as biochemical puppets of the deterministic yet partly random firing of the synapses in our brains. But he also holds that the mind is at distance from the brain so that we can "grab the strings" of the biochemical puppet master by behaving differently. Contradictory statements about free will certainly get applause: They allow people to take credit for their virtues and blame the outside world for their vices. But do they bring us closer to the truth?"

"They don't, Albert. In my time, we call those playing both sides of the field sophists. Some even say they are snakes because they speak with split tongues."

"Snakes are purposely untruthful, Epicurus. They lie. Harris doesn't lie. He merely runs into cognitive conflicts because he dives deeper than most others into existential matters."

"But you can't accuse me of being a sophist or a snake because I don't deny free will."

"I certainly won't, Epicurus. But still, your gods are a handful! Not only do they encourage you to party hard but also to play dice with their swerving atoms. I have a more platonic picture of the divine."

"Tell me."

"The divine beauty reveals itself in the mathematical equations that rule our universe. *That* is the Secret of the Old One. Mathematics is too beautiful to be merely human; it is sacred reality!"

"Plato and I never got along. Your reality seems merely an abstraction of the undeniable but inexplicable instantaneous experience."

"Oh, you . . . audacious you, challenging Plato! In my time, his premise of a mind-independent truth is still considered unassailable."

"But, Albert, why would you externalize the truth? Truth is what you are. Your and my existence is inner truth: the truth that is oppositeless existence."

"Oh dear . . . I didn't know you were a nondualist too, Epicurus."

"I wasn't, but that was over two thousand years ago. I had some time to think about it. And it fits with my philosophy, which allows people to do what feels right. It's okay to choose for joy because, contrary to certain spiritual teachings, Tao doesn't equal joy. Joy has an opposite, so it isn't Tao. Enlightenment certainly brings *joy, though, and even more so, inner peace.*

"Those on the brink of enlightenment shouldn't be disappointed or discouraged when they still find themselves hurting and distressed sometimes. Enlightened people are still human. That is why the Epicurean way of life is consistent with nondualistic insight. When you celebrate life with an enlightened mind, you naturally integrate virtues such as moderation, compassion, and foresight. Tao isn't egocentric, unmeasured, or cynical, nor is Epicureanism. The boundless mind knows its boundaries—and it certainly knows how to love."

"Well said, Epicurus. That was quite the monologue! Your throat must be dry now. I'm an empirical scientist rather than a talker. We should put your theories to the test. Why don't we open that bottle of wine already and talk about something lighter than philosophy? Find out what it feels like. For instance, how about those Olympic games?"

"I thought you'd never ask! Philosophy is only useful insofar as it heals the soul. And a glass of wine can do wonders to the soul as well."

"Prosit, Epicurus. Here's to truth and joy!"

"Cheers, Albert!"

3

NONDUALITY AND REASON

In the winter of 2021, my wife and I visited "Banksy: Genius or Vandal? An Unauthorized Exhibition" in Brussels, Belgium. I belong to those who consider him a genius and admire his work. Banksy is a famously elusive anti-establishment graffiti artist who sprays his work on walls in public urban settings, instantly turning those walls into priceless pieces of art.

On his website, Banksy denounces unauthorized exhibitions like the one we visited in Brussels as fake, turning himself inevitably into the kind of property-concerned establishment figure he condemns. It shows that no one can remain on the ethical sidelines and "pure" in our nondual world because living means participating in our shared existence. But that is not why I bring him up here.

I tell Banksy's story to illustrate two essential facets of nondualistic metaphysics: *identity* and *inconceivability*. It is a different approach to the same nonduality discussed previously. *Identity* and *inconceivability* are notions that help you grasp nondualistic metaphysics.

Banksy works in the shadows and anonymously: He is a mystery. We know from documentaries and his website that he is British and a *he*. Whenever a new work that might be attributed to him pops up, a frenzied analysis ensues to see if it's "a real Banksy" or, perhaps, merely an imitation in his style.

Imagine that one early morning at 4 a.m., two Banksy-style graffiti are found in subway entrances in the busy streets of Stockholm, Sweden, and Madrid, Spain: two cities in the same time zone a four-hour flight apart. Numerous people in both cities can confirm that even at 1 a.m., the graffiti weren't there yet, so the works must have been sprayed at roughly the same time, somewhere between 1 and 4 a.m.

Art connoisseurs swiftly conclude that at least one of the two graffiti pieces is fake. Of course, the key issue is the artist's *identity*: At least one graffiti isn't made by Banksy himself. There must have been two different artists since they weren't at the same location when they created the graffiti: One of the artists' *properties* was different, so they couldn't have been identical.

But now, in our fictional thought experiment, footage surfaces of what happened at the subway entrance in Madrid: A woman is seen spraying and fleeing the scene. The authorities recognize the lady, and when they confront her, she confesses she made the graffiti. The art experts are now convinced that the graffiti in Stockholm is Banksy's: It follows his style completely. Banksy's announcement of the Stockholm piece on his Instagram may also be a clue.

Perhaps unknowingly, the art experts have applied a principle of rational thought to identify the artist: the law of identity of indiscernibles, also known as the law of identity. Gottfried Wilhelm Leibniz, the genius seventeenth-century polymath and rationalist philosopher, is credited for articulating this rational thought principle. It goes like this: "No two substances should resemble each other entirely." The *artist* is the "substance" the art experts wished to identify. To do so, they compared properties or attributes like style, location, time, and Instagram announcements.[11]

The first takeaway is that we can use the principle of identity to identify something or someone through attributes, even when *what or whom* we identify is a mystery.

But when is Banksy no longer a mystery? Imagine that a journalist publishes his first and family name, place of residence, and some clearly recognizable photos. Banksy is no longer anonymous. But how many attributes of Banksy do we need to know before considering his mystery solved? There are endless "Banksy facts" to be discovered. Who are his parents? When was he born? Which molecules does his body consist of? Where does he go on vacation?

No matter how many Banksy attributes we know, such facts will never entirely tell us who or what Banksy truly *is*. Banksy's properties cannot reveal his essence—which is his existence. This is not only the case for Banksy but also for you, me, and literally everything. Attributes can potentially identify everything and everyone, but no number of attributes can reveal the ultimate essence—what exists, what truly is. The mystery of existence is that facts don't reveal reality.

Who can solve the mystery of Banksy's existence in our thought experiment? Undoubtedly, Banksy knows more Banksy facts than anyone else. But even Banksy doesn't know all the endless facts about himself. Conceptually, Banksy must remain somewhat of a mystery even to himself.

So, how *does* one know oneself, if not conceptually? Can we solve the mystery of our existence? The answer is *yes!* The way to do it is so simple that many people are unaware it's possible. Numerous people spend much of their life trying to "find

---

[11] The words *attributes* and *properties* have different connotations. In a dualistic paradigm, people assign *attributes,* while *properties* are characteristics of reality. However, since reality isn't available in a nondualistic paradigm, people must ultimately assign both. Accordingly, I alternate these words as if they were synonymous.

themselves," to "figure out who they really are," and often feel they don't fully succeed. For their self-discovery, they may pass through phases of experimentation and exploration, indulgence and sacrifice. But "who they are" is so close to them that they completely miss it as if they were looking for their glasses while wearing them.

You know yourself by simply existing. Your immediate first-person experience of *what it's like to be* tells you incessantly and unequivocally who and what you are—but only strictly before anything of *what it's like to be* "detaches" itself in the form of concepts from your present experience. You cannot avoid knowing your existence because unconceived knowledge and existence are identical! They have the same properties when we consider them from a first-person viewpoint—as we should since there is no experience without a subject.

You know your existence entirely, but exclusively in a pre-conceptual, unconceived way: as immediate experience. Whenever you conceive your experience and possibly label it with words, that conceived knowledge no longer contains your real existence because it has lost its immediacy. It has become merely a memory of real existence. Real existence is inconceivable.

The second takeaway is that existence can be *identified* by its attributes and *known* by simply recognizing that it equals your immediate experience—of which you can become aware by simply turning your attention to it. But existence cannot be *captured* into concepts. Real existence is inconceivable, so facts don't reveal it.

Once you realize that your existence is identical to your present experience, which is the same as *what it's like to be*, you can easily verify that existence is inconceivable. For example, try to conceive, to put into words what it's like to smell cinnamon or see the color blue. No words can ever convey the essence of such subjective experiences, even though you probably know them. We know that others also smell

3. NONDUALITY AND REASON

cinnamon and see blue, but if they experience it as we do is unknowable because real experience is private.

Understanding the inconceivability of existence and experience is central to fathoming nondualistic metaphysics. So, let me illustrate it with another example. The *rainbow* goes from red, orange, green, blue, indigo, to the last visible color, violet. We know there is ultraviolet too, but we can't see it.[12]

Butterflies, however, see more colors than humans, including ultraviolet. They have four types of visual cone cells instead of three like humans. Their rainbow is wider than ours! Imagine that a butterfly could talk. The cordial butterfly might warn us about an ultraviolet stain on our shirt or draw our attention to a beautiful ultraviolet flower.

But no matter how intelligent and eloquent the butterfly is and how much we do our best to understand it, we will never know what it's like to see *ultraviolet color* because we have never experienced it. The concept of *ultraviolet color* is an empty label because it doesn't tell us *how* the butterfly perceives ultraviolet—otherwise, the butterfly's words could convey the experience to humans.

But the words yellow, blue, and cinnamon aroma are also empty labels that do not transport real experience. The meaning of concepts, facts, and attributes comes *uniquely* from the receiver's memory—memories of what existence is like, for example, what it's like to see yellow or blue. And such meaning from memory arises *exclusively* in the present moment. Again, we categorically lack access to *what* exists—to reality—because existence is inconceivable. We only know what existence *is like* and can recognize and identify its phenomena by comparing them with our memories.

As Banksy solves the mystery of his existence not by gathering more facts about himself but by simply paying attention to the experience of what it's like to be, so does the

---

[12] *Blacklight* is visible and mostly UV, so it might seem we can see UV light. However, the visible portion of blacklight is not UV.

butterfly example show that whatever the mind conceives doesn't reveal reality. Only the present experience that *is* the conscious mind is real. *What* that conscious mind conceives is not real because it remains meaningless as long as it is not experienced by a conscious mind in the present.

Who is Banksy? Are you? Am I? Without exception, our existence is our instantaneous experience *before* we conceive it. We can only know *how* our—and all—existence is because once we try to capture *what* existence is, we have to conceive something, and whatever we conceive is merely a memory of *how* something was. Memories of instantaneous experience can never contain real instantaneous experience. So, what or who we are remains conceptually a mystery: the mystery that we entirely know because it is the mystery that we *are*—our instantaneous experience.

Reality is another word for *what* existence is. The difference between real experience and reality is that the former is mind-dependent and the latter mind-independent. The word *reality* has the connotation of something reified, objectified, substantialized. Real existence is a world with a subject and reality a world without. Reason summons us to be precise with words to avoid confusion. Hence, we should not call our experience—or the *facts* we derive from it—reality. We cannot know what exists because existence is inconceivable. So, neither can we know reality—at all! This is perhaps the most counterintuitive of all the rational conclusions of nondualistic metaphysics.

The implications of our lack of access to reality are staggering. Our belief in a readily available reality is so deeply ingrained in our minds that we almost automatically reject these implications. Here are a few examples:
- ✓ *Nothing* anyone has ever thought, written, or talked *about* exists.
- ✓ Scientific experiments, measurements, mathematical equations, and the laws of physics do *not* reveal reality.

3. NONDUALITY AND REASON

- ✓ Objective knowledge is unavailable to the human mind.
- ✓ Your *self* does not exist.
- ✓ Other people and creatures don't exist.
- ✓ Objects don't exist, including the ground under your feet and the sun that comes up in the morning.
- ✓ Your body does not exist.
- ✓ Submicroscopic objects like atoms, molecules, and quantum objects don't exist.
- ✓ Time and space do not exist.
- ✓ Cause and effect do not exist.

Everything we normally take for reality is imagined only. What we tend to see as reality is nothing but memories: abstractions of experience patterns that our minds make for themselves and other minds. These *concepts* have no meaning whatsoever beyond our minds. For example, we may see a blue sky. But what is blue about it? How we experience it. There is nothing blue about a sky that is not being perceived. Precisely the same holds for everything else: Nothing is *what* we know because everything is *how* we know it.

The culprit of our susceptibility to dualism is not our lack of intelligence: Some of the most brilliant people in history were avowed dualists. Rather, it is evolution. Evolution has equipped us with conscious minds for its biological purposes: to distinguish ourselves from the rest of the world, pursue life's catalysts and avoid life's threats. The central task of our conscious minds is to perceive and evaluate these distinctions, perform mental simulations on them, and, based on the findings, put our motor system (nerves, muscles, . . .) into action. Since conceiving and evaluating differences is its central task, it is hard for the conscious mind to recognize and acknowledge that the distinctions it perceives don't exist beyond itself.

But even when you *do* recognize the dualistic illusion and its pervasiveness, you may still say, "So what? Duality is an illusion, but, as you said yourself, we cannot conceive the world in any other way. So, we might as well assume that the world is dualistic." In other words, the question is whether dualism has any downsides and, if so, if they can be remedied by nondualism. I turned to OpenAI's *ChatGPT* to get an overview of the general views on these questions.

[Me] What are the downsides of philosophical dualism?

[ChatGPT] Philosophical dualism is the belief that there are two fundamentally different kinds of substances or entities in the world, such as mind and matter, or spirit and body. While there are some philosophical arguments in favor of dualism, there are also several downsides to this perspective:
- ✓ Lack of empirical evidence: Dualism is a metaphysical concept that cannot be directly observed or measured. This makes it difficult to provide empirical evidence in support of dualism, and it may be considered a speculative or unfalsifiable theory.
- ✓ The interaction problem: Dualism raises the question of how two fundamentally different substances (such as mind and body) can interact with each other. This is known as the interaction problem, and it has been a major challenge for dualist theories throughout history.
- ✓ The problem of individuation: Dualism raises questions about how two fundamentally different substances can be distinguished from one another, and how they are related to each other. This can be a difficult problem to solve, and it may lead to further metaphysical speculation and debate.
- ✓ The problem of mental causation: Dualism suggests that mental events can have causal effects on physical events, which raises questions about the nature of causation and the relationship between mind and body. Some philosophers have argued that this is a problematic concept, and that it may be difficult to provide a satisfactory account of mental causation within a dualist framework.

3. NONDUALITY AND REASON

- ✓ The problem of survival: Dualism raises questions about the relationship between the mind and the body after death, and whether the mind or soul can survive without the body. This is a difficult problem to address, and it may lead to conflicting beliefs about the nature of the afterlife and the existence of an immortal soul.

[Me] How can nondualism resolve these issues?

[ChatGPT] There are several ways in which nondualism may offer solutions to some of the issues raised by dualism:
- ✓ Empirical evidence: Nondualism is often based on empirical evidence from fields such as physics or neuroscience, which can be directly observed and tested. This can provide a more concrete basis for understanding the nature of reality, and may make it easier to avoid speculative or unfalsifiable theories.
- ✓ The interaction problem: Nondualism avoids the interaction problem by positing that there is only one fundamental substance or entity in the world, rather than two or more distinct substances that need to interact with each other.
- ✓ The problem of individuation: Nondualism suggests that all things are ultimately interconnected and part of a larger whole, which can help to solve the problem of individuation by emphasizing the unity of all things.
- ✓ The problem of mental causation: Nondualism can offer a more unified account of causation, which avoids the problem of mental causation by positing that all events are ultimately caused by the same fundamental substance or entity.
- ✓ The problem of survival: Nondualism suggests that the mind and body are not separate entities, but rather different aspects of the same underlying reality. This can help to address the problem of survival by suggesting that the mind and body are not separate after death, but rather continue to exist as part of the same unified

reality.

[Me] What are the advantages of nondualism for mental well-being?

[ChatGPT] Nondualism, which is the belief in the fundamental unity of all things, can have several advantages for mental well-being:
- ✓ Reduced anxiety: Nondualism suggests that there is no fundamental separation between oneself and the rest of the world, which can help to reduce feelings of anxiety and isolation. By recognizing the interconnectedness of all things, individuals may feel a sense of belonging and connection with the world around them.
- ✓ Increased mindfulness: Nondualism encourages individuals to be present in the moment and to recognize the interconnectedness of all things. This can promote mindfulness and awareness, which are associated with improved mental health outcomes.
- ✓ Reduced ego-centered thinking: Nondualism emphasizes the idea that the self is not a separate entity, but rather part of a larger whole. This can help individuals to recognize and reduce ego-centered thinking, which is often associated with negative emotions such as jealousy, resentment, and anger.
- ✓ Increased empathy and compassion: Nondualism encourages individuals to recognize the interconnectedness of all things, which can help to cultivate a sense of empathy and compassion for others. This can promote positive social relationships and reduce feelings of isolation and loneliness.
- ✓ Increased acceptance: Nondualism suggests that all things are ultimately part of the same underlying reality, which can help individuals to accept and come to terms with difficult or challenging experiences. This can promote resilience and emotional well-being.

In addition to ChatGPT's impressive responses, I see the following downsides of dualism:
- ✓ Dualism projects an external truth to which human value is secondary. This may drive individuals to excessive perfectionism. In secular-dualistic cultures, it may also lead to toxic utopian ideologies.
- ✓ Secular dualism erodes the foundations of reason as a healthy societal principle. The external "objective" reality seemingly trumps "subjective" reason, creating an intellectual vacuum in which irrationality can thrive.
- ✓ Secular-dualistic mindsets and cultures are poorly equipped to deal with *guilt*. *Chapter 4* elaborates on this.

EXISTENTIAL REASON

We have now approached the inconceivable nonduality, commonly known as Tao, from different angles: metaphysics, introspection, and the rational principle of identity. The purpose is to give you pointers to Tao so that you may find it. Before addressing Tao from yet another angle and applying nondualistic insight to real-world issues, we will probe deeper into the relationship between reason and nonduality.

There are numerous ways to explain nonduality. Each way can add to your susceptibility of "getting it." Even when they confuse you, that confusion may be helpful too. Nonduality tends to confuse because it is counterintuitive. The mind usually *conceives* to understand, but the nonduality can only be understood when unconceived.

In this subchapter, we will investigate *existential reason*: the kind of reason that recognizes *unconceived* knowledge, as opposed to dualistic reason, which only considers *conceived* knowledge—concepts. Existential reason goes beyond the imaginary objective world and explores the empirical roots of reason in instantaneous subjective experience.

Dualistic science is concerned with mind-independent truth, distrusts metaphysics because it is subjective, and hopes to objectify the subjective experience via scientific methods. However, nondualistic metaphysics entails that *all* knowledge is subjective. Even the assumption that metaphysics is unscientific is ultimately a subjective metaphysical assumption—a self-defeating one, might I add.

If we re-embrace metaphysics as the first philosophy, we can rediscover the power of reason to answer a host of existential questions, individual and collective, big and small. Nondualism means we no longer idolize reality but put human experience at the center of our knowledge. Existential reason makes science and subjectivity compatible.

※

What is the one thing most Western philosophers agree on? I invite you to ponder this question for a moment. It is telling that there is so much they *don't* agree on and passionately discuss in sometimes hard-to-follow debates. I am not a professional philosopher but an engineer intrigued by philosophy. As a philosophical outsider, I have always been struck by the lack of agreement in Western philosophy on metaphysics—topics like reality, knowledge, and truth. We are all humans living on the same planet. Why is so little settled in Western philosophy?

In contrast, there is more consensus in Eastern philosophy. Leaving the religious interpretations aside, when we ask people of Buddhist, Taoist, or Hindu persuasion what reality, truth, and knowledge are made of, many will give a relatively clear-cut answer: Reality, truth, and knowledge are *one* and their perceived manifestation as separate creatures, objects, and "mind content" is an illusion. Admittedly, even for Eastern people it is hard to fathom what that means, not to mention that many of them still have dualistic philosophical and religious tenets. But the higher level of agreement in the East makes its metaphysics seem more convincing.

Still, there is one thing most Western philosophers—and scientists—*do* agree on: that conceptual knowledge is never beyond doubt, never certain. Descartes famously said that all knowledge was doubtful except for the fact that he was thinking. The Cartesian definition of thought, you may recall, "What happens in me such that I am immediately conscious of it, insofar as I am conscious of it," shows that his "thinking" is not only cognition but the entire conscious experience. He is certain that he *is* a conscious mind but uncertain about the *concepts* his conscious mind produces.

Another philosophical superstar is David Hume. With different arguments, he also concludes that conceptual knowledge cannot offer certainty about the world. His insights in a nutshell: *Reason* is not absolute but rooted in the human passions, and no prediction can ever be certain because we cannot exclude the possibility that we have overseen something that ought to have changed our prediction. The latter is known as Hume's "problem of induction."[13]

Hume doesn't contest the value of, say, the equations representing the laws of physics or the predictions that we make with them but merely points out that even the most brilliant physics equation cannot ever be considered ultimate, final knowledge.

Modern science agrees with Descartes and Hume that conceptual knowledge, even when scientific, can never be absolutely certain. Karl Popper's *falsification criterion* is widely used to distinguish scientific from unscientific knowledge. Popper, a twentieth-century Austrian-British philosopher, explains that scientific knowledge must be verifiable by a replicable experiment but can never be proved beyond doubt. As long as an experiment doesn't falsify the knowledge, it can

---

[13] Hume's skepticism is famously summarized as 'Hume's Fork': Empirical *matters of facts* don't provide certainty because of the problem of induction, and rational *relations of ideas* don't provide certainty because reason is rooted in the passions and results from custom and habit.

be considered scientific knowledge.

The intrinsic uncertainty of conceptual knowledge is one of the rare instances where Eastern and Western philosophy agree. Both recognize that we are barking up the wrong tree when we demand certainty from concepts. Everything we can ever speak, write, or think about are concepts, and conceptual certainty about the world is categorically unavailable.[14]

Ever since Plato, Western thought typically distinguishes knowledge from opinion and belief by its certainty. However, Hume showed that certainty about the world is not available—earning him the *skeptic* label. But instead of acknowledging that Humean skepticism turns *all* conceived knowledge ultimately into mere beliefs, the West remains adamant about finding conceptual certainty and distrusts all knowledge that can't be empirically verified—because it hasn't given up on the dualistic hope of finding the mind-independent truth. Due to our dualism, the rise of empiricism since Hume has come at the expense of *reason*. Let me explain why nondualism can restore reason's role.

The belief in a mind-independent truth marks Western thought. Our ideal is objectivity, which can be achieved by empirical verification, mathematics, and deductive logic.

What is the difference between deduction and induction? Both are fundamental reasoning methods used to draw conclusions or make inferences. The main difference between these methods is how they arrive at their conclusions. Deduction is a logical process that moves from general principles to specific conclusions, while induction is a process that moves from specific observations to general conclusions. The famous examples of the two types of logic are:
- ✓ Deduction: "All men are mortal. Socrates is a man.

---

[14] Fortunately, this doesn't mean no certainty is available to us. Descartes and Eastern thought point us in a different direction than concepts to find such certainty. The only certainty we have is the certainty we *are*: the undisputable immediate conscious experience known as Tao.

Therefore, Socrates is mortal."
- ✓ Induction: "Since all the swans I have seen are white, all swans must be white."

Hume's problem of induction tells us that the latter is not true: We might still find a black swan afterward. Ever since Hume, induction has been perceived as tainted: unscientific and unreliable.

But why are logical deduction, mathematics, and empirical proof considered scientific and rational? Because we implicitly or explicitly hold that, unlike specific observations, mathematical axioms, general principles of deductive logic, and empirical proof *are* imbued with some objective, mind-independent truth.

However, Hume also clarified that all human mental endeavors, including deductive logic, mathematics, and empirical verification, are based on the passions—on custom and habit rather than absolute truth. And in a nondualistic paradigm, *all* knowledge has to be empirical because it *must* represent experience: Even mathematical axioms, general principles of deductive logic, and empirical proof's pertinence are rooted in subjectivity.[15]

Why do we put so much trust in empirical verification and mathematical equations? Nonduality implies that not reality but *nondual, singular experience* is the argument for their validity. In our conscious minds, we are continuously experiencing that there is a single world. Two ears, two eyes, a nose, a skin: The information from our senses is combined into a single world image in ways so familiar that we no longer recognize it as an empirical fact. And we share that same single world with other people.

If we experienced multiple parallel worlds instead, empirical evidence would be meaningless because experimental

---

[15] So, technically, the problem of induction also affects the validity of mathematical, deductive, and empirical knowledge.

verification could be successful in one world and unsuccessful in the other. And mathematics works with equations. It surmises that both sides of the equation refer to the same single world.

The underlying assumption of rational thought is *also* the singularity of subjective experience. If we didn't experience the world in a singular way, it would be perfectly fine for Banksy to have certain properties in one world and simultaneously another set of properties in a parallel world. We wouldn't be able to identify the artist Banksy. Meaningful statements could be true in one world and not true in another. Such parallel worlds would be incomprehensible to us. We can't be sure reality is one, but we *are* sure we can't understand a world that is *not* one.

So, the *empirical* fact upholding the rules of rational thought is Tao's present singularity which we can continuously and instantly verify in our subjective experience. We needn't pit empiricism against reason because both are empirical, and reality is inaccessible. Suppose we use the nondualistic one-world paradigm instead of mind-reality dualism as an argument for reason. In that case, we can extend the scope of reason to existential areas where no empirical verification is possible or feasible.

So, while a nondualistic paradigm leads to recognizing exactly the same types of valid justifications for knowledge as a dualistic paradigm, namely mathematics, deductive logic, and empirical proof *when possible*, it *additionally* holds that the rules of rational thought can be used to *induce* rational knowledge *when useful*.

Thus, nonduality dramatically increases the scope of rational thought in our lives. There are vital existential matters beyond empirical verification, such as:
- ✓ Individuals' existential matters like subjectivity and spirituality.
- ✓ Collective existential matters like metaphysics and ideology.

3. NONDUALITY AND REASON

Nondualism recognizes that conceptual knowledge is never absolute and that reason is rooted in Tao: sovereign, necessarily true present experience. Truth feelings transpire instantaneously, beyond our control, but we can trust them better when our beliefs are rational. To distinguish nondualistic reason from classical dualistic reason, we can call it *existential reason*—reason all the same but firmly rooted in our inescapable subjectivity and valid even before experimental verification.

Classical Cartesian reason is dualistic, and Hume rightly pointed out that it doesn't lead to certainty. But nonduality sustains existential reason that finds its certainty in the undeniable instantaneous essence of all conscious minds. Nondualistic existential reason answers Humean skepticism, which impedes a rational approach to existential issues. The difference between dualistic reason and existential reason is that the latter allows us to *reasonably judge*. Existential reason doesn't lead to undoubtable solutions but sustains meaningful, solution-driven, civic debate.

Existential matters and practical engineering have in common that we sometimes must make decisions when empirical verification is only partially feasible. In such cases, we are bound to use reason to infer truthful, reliable knowledge. Reason is all about clarity, getting the facts straight. How do we do that, getting the facts straight?

Engineers are continuously challenged to do precisely that because if we don't, bridges collapse, computers crash, rockets explode, and cars end up in a ditch. Engineers do lots of testing, but we don't have the luxury of testing every real-world scenario. The solutions we design are usually larger-scale versions of what we have tested on a smaller scale. We *induce* our knowledge even though it doesn't lead to the holy grail of conceptual certainty. But it's the best we can do! And when done well, it is compelling. Moreover, from my experience as an engineer, I can confirm that rigorous rational thinking is far more demanding than merely lazily tendering scientific doubt and waiting for empirical evidence.

Getting the facts straight means that we aim for meaningful statements (steel type A is okay for our bridge, but type B is not), non-contradictory statements (any steel with properties A is of type A, and any with properties B of type B), mutually exclusive statements (one type of steel cannot be of type A and B simultaneously), and insist on solid argumentation for statements (steel type A is okay for our bridge because it is stronger than B).

The official philosophical terms for these principles of rational thought are:
- ✓ The law of non-contradiction: Two meaningful contradictory statements cannot both be true within the same context.
- ✓ The law of the excluded middle: A meaningful statement is either true or not.
- ✓ The law of identity (of indiscernibles): Two substances that share all properties are the same substance. As discussed before in the Banksy example.
- ✓ The principle of sufficient reason: We don't assume anything without a justification that respects the other principles of rational thought.

These principles may sound theoretical but formalize something quite practical: common sense. Have you ever wondered why this commodity is in such short supply these days? I blame it on secular dualism, which snubs our inescapable subjectivity. Nondualism revindicates common sense because the sovereign inner truth is available to all.

※

Not only scientific dualists but also spiritual dualists can be suspicious of reason. When seekers understand reason as the antithesis of spirituality, they reveal their implicit dualism of worldly versus other-worldly matters. In contrast, existential reason allows us to bridge the divide between spirituality,

3. NONDUALITY AND REASON

reason, and science because it builds on their shared nondual origins. Nondualistic metaphysics leads to existential reason, and existential reason leads to nondualistic metaphysics. Tao's inner truth sustains spiritual experience, cognition, and scientific experiment alike.

How does our mind come from its undivided inner truth to the feelings of *right* and *wrong*? The answer is simple: through our beliefs. But when we believe something to be profoundly truthful, we could be mistaken since we may be misinformed or under the spell of an illusion. We can trust our inner truth because it is always there when we are conscious. But we cannot necessarily trust our feelings of right and wrong because our beliefs could be inaccurate.

Since no mind-independent reality is available as a truth reference in the nondualistic worldview, we end up with reason as the viable method to ensure our beliefs are truthful. Rational beliefs are as truthful as conceptual knowledge can get. Those who haven't yet learned how to shape their beliefs to produce feelings they can trust will likely end up disappointed on their spiritual journey. *Chapter 4* discusses false spiritual promises.

※

Existential reason is key to rational nondualism, so here is a summary of how we moved from the prevailing Western secular-dualistic mindset to the proposed amalgam of "Eastern" nondualism and "Western" reason.
- ✓ Typical dualistic Western thought considers the mind subjective and reality objective.
- ✓ Ever since Hume laid bare the subjective roots of reason, Western thought has favored "objective" empiricism over "subjective" rationalism.
- ✓ Nondualistic metaphysics resolves the paradox between mind and reality because it acknowledges that the world only exists as the subject-object unity known as Tao. Tao is unconceived knowledge. The mind splits it into

- ✓ Since both empiricism and reason are rooted in unconceived experience, there is no longer a contradiction between "subjective" reason and "objective" empirical science. Hence, we can trust reason in matters beyond empirical science.
- ✓ Existential reason is reason predicated on nonduality and restores the principles of rational thought that have fallen into disuse since Hume. Unlike secular-dualistic reason, existential reason allows reasonable judgment.

THE TREE

We identified the mysterious Banksy by his properties and can do the same with Tao. From the first-person perspective, Tao shares all properties with change, the present, existence, and the conscious mind. So, they are all identical.

Such perplexing conclusions can be hard to deal with. Even Zen monks need ten to twenty years to grasp nonduality. The Japanese word *satori* indicates the epiphany that the conceptual world and self are imaginary. Satori is the purpose of the Zen Buddhist monks' curriculum, as Daisetsu Teitaro (D.T.) Suzuki (1870-1966), a pioneer teacher of Zen to the West, explains in his 1934 book *Introduction to Zen Buddhism*. Once satori is realized, the mind is ready to fathom the present as one with the mind and the whole world—as the entity, the *substance* known as Tao.

You can readily probe the depth of your nondualistic awareness. For example, you could ask yourself, "What is my consciousness?" Once you have found an answer, you can ask yourself what the *opposite* is of your understanding of consciousness. Many suppose it's *unconsciousness*, or something like blackness, silence, or emptiness. However, unconsciousness is the opposite of the *concept* of consciousness,

3. NONDUALITY AND REASON

which isn't *real* consciousness. To conceive unconsciousness, you still need to be conscious.

The difference between the concept of consciousness and real consciousness is that the latter doesn't have an opposite. So, as long as you feel your consciousness has an opposite, you haven't yet discovered your real existence: Tao. Lao Tzu's wisdom never grows old: "The Tao that can be told is not the true Tao."

Another thought experiment to test your nondualistic discernment is so famous that it is almost commonplace: "When a tree falls in a forest, and there is no witness, does it make a sound?" The answer often goes along the lines of "Yes! Of course the tree makes a sound. The absence of a witness doesn't change the objective fact of sound waves. We could measure the sound or record it and play it back later to confirm that there was a sound."

Unfortunately, this answer is irrational because it misconceives what *sound* is. Is sound the same as sound waves, eardrums, nerve signals to the brain's auditory cortex, or a number of decibels? No. Sound is a subjective experience. So, there is no sound when a tree falls in a forest without a witness.

Sound without a mind is like spaghetti without pasta or an ocean without water. Considering that there is a sound because there *could* have been a witness, even though the thought experiment clearly states there wasn't, is a contradiction. It surmises reality in hypothetical, imaginary world constructs.

The belief in mind-independent knowledge, of falling trees makings sounds without witnesses, is faith-based—religious—because it requires extra-sensory perception and the mind's supernatural ability to cross over to mystical realms. Such beliefs always violate the law of non-contradiction by presuming knowledge of the unknowable. Paradoxically, knowledge of reality, *objective* knowledge, is an esoteric and occult premise.

Yet, Western thought is profoundly dualistic. Ever since

Plato and Aristotle, we believe that reality and truth are removed from the subjective experience and only discoverable by painstaking thought, mathematical analysis, and experiment. Dualistic science has been incredibly successful: The quest for "objective" knowledge has spurred our invaluable technological and scientific progress. Its successes discourage admitting the deeply rooted flaw in Western thought.

Albert Einstein is perhaps the most distinguished of all scientists. His relativity theories reveal that we don't need to conceive absolute space and time to understand physics. Nonetheless, he is a monistic dualist. His deservedly legendary status may have kept us from noticing that his metaphysical tenets are . . . irrational! If a scientist of his stature believes in mind-independent reality, who would dare to challenge it?

Einstein's belief in truth independent of the mind is on record multiple times. For example, a 1930 dialogue with Rabindranath Tagore, an Indian, Nobel-Prize-winning polymath, author, and philosopher, went as follows:

[. . .]

[Einstein] . . . truth, then, or beauty, is not independent of man?

[Tagore] No.

[Einstein] If there would be no humans anymore, the Apollo of Belvedere would no longer be beautiful?

[Tagore] No.

[Einstein] I agree with regard to this conception of beauty, but not with regard to truth.

[Tagore] Why not? Truth is realized through man.

[Einstein] I cannot prove that my conception is right, but

3. NONDUALITY AND REASON

that is my religion.

[Tagore] Beauty is in the ideal of perfect harmony which is in the universal being; truth the perfect comprehension of the universal mind. We individuals approach it through our own mistakes and blunders, through our accumulated experience, through our illumined consciousness—how, otherwise, can we know truth?

[Einstein] I cannot prove scientifically that truth must be conceived as a truth that is valid independent of humanity, but I believe it firmly. [. . .] Anyway, if there is a reality independent of man there is also a truth relative to this reality; and in the same way the negation of the first engenders a negation of the existence of the latter.

[Tagore] Truth, which is one with the universal being, must essentially be human, otherwise whatever we individuals realize as true can never be called truth—at least the truth which is described as scientific and can only be reached through the process of logic, in other words, by an organ of thoughts which is human. According to Indian philosophy, there is Brahman the absolute truth, which cannot be conceived by the isolation of the individual mind or described by words, but can only be realized by completely merging the individual in its infinity. But such a truth cannot belong to science. The nature of truth which we are discussing is an appearance—that is to say what appears to be true to the human mind and therefore is human, and may be called maya or illusion. [. . .]

[Einstein] Even in our everyday life we feel compelled to ascribe a reality independent of man to the objects we use. We do this to connect the experiences of our senses in a reasonable way. For instance, if nobody is in this house, that table remains where it is. [. . .] Our natural point of view in regard to the existence of truth apart from humanity cannot be explained or proved, but it is a belief which nobody can lack—no primitive beings even. We attribute to truth a super-human objectivity; it is indispensable for us, the reality which is independent of our existence and our experience and our mind—though we cannot say what it means.

[Tagore] Science has proved that the table as a solid object is an appearance, and therefore that which the human mind perceives as a table would not exist if that mind were naught. [. . .] There is the reality of paper, infinitely different from the reality of literature. For the kind of mind possessed by the moth, which eats that paper, literature is absolutely non-existent, yet for man's mind literature has a greater value of truth than the paper itself. In a similar manner, if there be some truth which has no sensuous or rational relation to the human mind it will ever remain as nothing so long as we remain human beings.

[Einstein] Then I am more religious than you are!

[. . .]

In his own words, Einstein *religiously* believes that conceiving a mind-independent truth and reality is indispensable. Tagore disagrees and considers that truth, reality, and mind are united in what he calls the universal being, before the mind imagines a separate truth and reality.

For Einstein to believe that a table exists independently of a witness—comparable to a falling tree making a sound without a witness—he must imagine what a hypothetical witness *would* perceive. Tagore's conclusion regarding the "witnessless" existence of tables and trees is more accurate since he avoids the contradiction of imaginary-yet-real witnesses.

Einstein considers the belief in a mind-independent reality essential for empirical science. The same argument might persuade many to accept the irrationality of mindless perception. The alternative, they fear, is the end of science and possibly chaos. They prefer religiously believing in divine reality because they dread the heretic void of nondualistic "atheism" or "a-realism."

The heresy accusation has always been dangerous: It sealed Galileo's fate of burning at the stake and got David Hume persecuted. I am not as presumptuous as to compare myself with them, but in our day and age, not believing in the objective knowledge revelation by reality's angels seriously impedes the prospects of an academic career. And although I don't aspire to an academic career, I do fear public opinion's wrath and ridicule. So, let me repeat that I am not an atheist with respect to supreme reality but an agnostic. To be precise, I hold that we cannot know reality but *do* know what it's like to be an aspect of reality. And we also *do* know that whatever we conceive is *not* reality.

"But," a monistic dualist like Einstein might argue, "you nondualists are even more irrational than I am. If the sound of the falling tree only exists when someone hears it, and you agree with Hume that nothing else exists 'in' the tree except for a bundle of sensations, then only those aspects of the tree that the witness pays attention to exist. The sounds of the tree, falling or not, its rustling leaves, smells, colors, texture, shape, and size: They swing in and out of existence by the mere blink of an eye or distractions by thoughts and other sensations that replace the tree in the witness's mind's attention."

This fierce argument might be another obstacle for dualists to relinquish their belief in subjectless perception. And it points to the only rational solution to this conundrum: the 180 degrees viewpoint shift of nondualistic metaphysics.

Tables and trees don't even exist *when* witnessed.

We have no access to *what* exists! Reality must remain a mystery. We only know impermanent experience, which is what it's like to be an inextricable part of reality's mystery. We don't know *what* reality is; we only know *how* reality is, what it's like to *be* reality. Our minds cannot pull themselves up by the bootstraps.

There is a logical-mathematical metaphor for the impossibility of conceiving the reality we are an aspect of. Kurt Gödel was born in 1906 in Brno, Czechia, then part of Austria-Hungary, and passed away in 1978. He was a philosopher, mathematician, and is widely recognized as one of the most important logicians in history. His reputation as a logician is owing to his 1931 publication of the so-called *incompletion theorems*, which demonstrate that no system axioms allow that same system's complete (mathematically proven) and consistent (proven to be without contradiction) description.

Likewise, that which is part of a system (the conscious mind) cannot conceptually know that system (reality). Stated otherwise, we have no access to necessary reasons for conceptual truth about the world. The best we can do are the sufficient reasons of rational thought.

When we abandon the hope of discovering a mind-independent truth, reason becomes conceptual knowledge's primary reference. Not reality but reason is the foundation of science, and existential reason helps to build rational beliefs and consensus in existential issues beyond empirical verification.

But not all knowledge needs to be rational. Once we have established rational beliefs, it is unnecessary to continue thinking for the sake of thought. Instead, we may behold and contemplate Tao's mystery for what it is, relish spirituality, whether secular or religious, give meaning to our lives—whatever that may mean for each of us individually—and celebrate life in general. Existential reason is a means to an end, not an end in itself.

With reality unavailable as a subject of inquiry, we must redefine the scope of science and rational thought: They concern what is mind-dependent. The mind-independent

3. NONDUALITY AND REASON

world is then reserved for religion and fiction. As long as they respect each other's territories, reason, science, and religion don't need to be antagonists.

I don't know enough about religion to calculate its balance of merits and drawbacks, so I don't see why people shouldn't believe in God—especially since existence is conceptually an intrinsic mystery. Yet, rational science should steer clear of faith-based religion, including the religious belief in reality.

Aristotle taught that metaphysics is the first philosophy and the foundation of all science. Nondualistic metaphysics isn't easy to understand but more rational than dualistic metaphysics. Nonduality entails that scientific knowledge is mind-dependent. This does *not* have repercussions on the scientific method but *does* expand the scope of rational thought. The fear of nondualism is ungrounded: Science can flourish even more when its roots are better understood.

Epicurus meets Lao Tzu

"Ni Hao."

"Excuse me? Hold on, let me start the translator app. Okay, could you repeat that, please?"

"Hello. My name is Lao Tzu. I'm sorry, but I will work with a translator in person. I like the old ways. That's also why I couldn't fly out to meet you in person."

"No problem. Better for the climate anyway. I'm Epicurus. . . . Are you sure your camera is on?"

"Oh! Excuse me . . . I always forget. Those darned Zoom calls . . ."

"Ah, now it works. You look in tip-top condition, Lao Tzu! It's an honor and delight."

"Thank you, Epicurus. So nice to meet you too. I heard you were quite the Dionysian, but it doesn't show."

"*Don't believe everything they say.*"

"When an Epicurean meets a Dionysian, what sound is heard?"

"*. . . And please don't confuse me with your koans! I was warned you would do that. We have to focus here because we have a lot of terrain to cover.*"

"We'll have it your way. ♪Much more than this . . . ♪I did it . . ."

"*Please don't sing* My Way! *They told me you would do that too.*"

"Sorry, hard to resist . . . my philosophy just lets me go with the flow, and we have such a good vibe, Epicurus! From reading your work, I gather you're not an explicit nondualist like me, but you don't seem adamantly against the idea either."

"*I also feel we get along well, Lao Tzu. I'd offer you some wine, but you aren't here with me.*"

"I would have refused—just tea for me. I miss the enzyme to digest alcohol. My blood pressure rises dangerously when I drink it. It's almost like poison to me."

"*No problem. Shows the difficulty of universal ethical rules. What's good for one person might be bad for the other.*"

"Nice pivot to philosophy, Epicurus! And may I say, not in a shy way."

"*. . . But there is a universal observation on which we can base our ethics.*"

"Being?"

"*That too, Lao Tzu, but I mean something more practical. Human consciousness universally perceives positive and negative value, although we value entirely different things. With few exceptions, even skeptics and nihilists like a drink when thirsty, and knowing what they value instantly defeats their skepticism and nihilism. Hence my philosophy. I invite people to accept without needless guilt that human behavior is motivated by pleasure and its opposite, by positive and negative experience, which is just another way of indicating human value. I must concede, though, that human value sounds better than pleasure. I'm probably not the best orator or politician you've ever met.*"

"I get your point, Epicurus. It's irrational to envision mind-independent, objective human value because human value can

3. NONDUALITY AND REASON

only transpire in subjective experience. I'm a hardline nondualist because dualism bewilders me. After talking with a dualist, I always need to do some calligraphy to calm down again."

"But I thought you liked koans? They are confusing too, aren't they?"

"True, but they are merely absurdities that point to the pre-conceptual truth, whereas dualistic philosophical systems are absurdities that claim to be conceptually accurate."

"But what does nondualism have to do with human value, Lao Tzu?"

"In nondualistic philosophical systems, human value is the only rational candidate for what moves the human mind. Anything else is dualistic because it implies that something outside the mind motivates it. Even the altruistic loving care of parents for their baby is spurred by pleasure. It is their pleasure to do something that feels totally natural and right. Ultimately, we're all driven by carrots and sticks, whether we like it or not."

"By Zeus! Carrots, sticks . . . you're not a great politician either! You and I, we just tell it as it is."

"The truth sets us free, Epicurus. But before you misunderstand me, that doesn't mean I see us humans as primitive animals. We were given our minds to understand our predicament so that we may rise above it. Perhaps the measure in which we are successful in doing so is precisely what distinguishes us from animals. Being more rational makes us more human. And I believe Tao's inner truth can show the way on our human journey."

"Thank you for your wisdom, Lao Tzu. You would have done well here in my ancient Greece. Your mind is sharp and rational."

"Oh, get out of here! You're making me blush. . . . But I do agree that reason travels easily across cultures because it doesn't require supernatural assumptions and routinely leads to better decision-making. And once you truly grasp it, you'll find that the inner truth, worldwide known under different names, leaves room for religious faith and easily crosses creeds and cultures as well. Reason leads to Tao, and Tao leads to reason."

". . . Which reminds me, I have another question. You speak of *grasping Tao. Is that what is meant by enlightenment?"*

"I'll state my case of which I'm certain. The enlightened mind fathoms nondualistic metaphysics."

"I see. So, do enlightened people believe the moon exists when no one looks at it? I promised Albert Einstein to ask you that."

"Does the moon disappear when you blink your eyes? Does it disappear when you are distracted and look at it without seeing? Does only the one crater you are focusing on exist? It is *absurd* to think that the moon becomes real by looking at it.

"But it is even more absurd to consider that the moon is real when you *don't* look at it since it is, in the words of David Hume, a bundle of sensations only. So, the moon exists merely as present experience and cannot be known to exist separately from that, not even *while* you look at it. The conclusion is that the moon cannot be known to exist at all.

"Instead, the moon is existence itself in that it is the same existence as your conscious mind. The moon doesn't exist separately from consciousness, and consciousness doesn't exist separately from the moon. Multiplicity is an illusion. *That* is nondualistic metaphysics."

"An illusion . . . what do you mean?"

"The moon doesn't *exist* because there aren't *many things*. There is only one inconceivable 'thing.' Mind, the present, change, *Tao*: It's all the same! And it's all there is. The enlightened mind understands this, Epicurus."

". . . Do you think I do, Lao Tzu? I seek a master who can tell me if I'm enlightened. The author told me you could help."

"It is simple. When you think you are enlightened, you may or may not be. But as long as you still doubt that you are enlightened, you are definitely not. So the question answers itself."

4

THE NATURE OF OUR NONDUALITY

Nondualistic metaphysics is simple: It consists of change and difference. Change is unconceived and real, while difference is conceived and imagined. Change, identical to the present and the conscious mind, is the unconceived knowledge of who we are and what the world is. We know existence entirely as unconceived knowledge, but once we conceive ourselves and the world, both become a mystery again.

So, what are we left with after this inexorable metaphysical analysis? What is the only mysterious "substance" that can ever be known to exist? The *present*, which is cognitively inexplicable but experientially without secrets and beyond doubt. Once you truly understand that the present is all there is and ever will be, and that nothing is separate from the present, you have grasped nondualistic metaphysics.

Although simple, nondualistic metaphysics is hard to accept because the human mind cannot help but conceive differences. Since nonduality also implies that we can't escape our human minds, we will continue to conceive differences and attribute value to them even after fathoming nondualistic metaphysics. These "differences" include people like you, me, and our loved ones. Realizing that, metaphysically speaking, people don't exist beyond our imagination doesn't make them less important. The world's creatures are expressions, *avatars* of Tao.

So, we exist in the world of change but live in the world of differences. Our existence does not equal our life because life has some permanence (meaning beyond the immediate present), while existence always changes. Life and existence are not identical because their properties differ. In Zen Buddhism, *samsara* alludes to *the world of differences*: life unto death and the sometimes-precarious human condition of recurring needs, desires, suffering, and contentment. As people, we live in samsara.

Can we escape from samsara? Can we transcend our humanity? Not if we truly accept that our existence is nondual. Precisely the unconditional surrender to the inescapable samsara is required for awakening to Tao's present oneness. Moreover, understanding samsara can make it a far more agreeable experience.

Differences may be imaginary, but we find value in them all the same—and that is okay! Nonduality invites us to celebrate our humanity instead of denying it. The human mind is naturally prone to passions, so our challenge is not to deny but to channel them. Reason can help us do so. More than two thousand years ago, the ancient Greek philosopher Epicurus already had excellent ideas of how to do that. This is why we find him sharing his insights in this book.

Even if you agree that nonduality is a captivating topic, you might still wonder why it matters beyond a stimulating mental exercise. This chapter illustrates its usefulness with present-day issues. Nondualism is more hands-on than dualistic philosophy. It is not about a theoretical objective world but our actual and practical way of living. Let's recap why existential reason has a wider scope than classical dualistic

reason:
- ✓ Nondualism rests on the observation that no one is a third person.
- ✓ Our being equals our first-person experience, which is in nothing different from the present or change.
- ✓ Since we are inextricably part of the world, we can only know *how* existence is but not *what* existence is. We lack access to reality, to mind-independent knowledge.
- ✓ Evolution has etched the dualistic illusion of cognitive access to reality into our conscious minds. Hence, nonduality cannot be grasped cognitively. Instead, it is an experience of insight, an awakening to the nonduality, the discovery of Tao: enlightenment.
- ✓ Enlightenment dispels the objective world illusion and reorients the mind toward present existence. Since the conscious experience arises spontaneously and immediately, its cause must remain beyond cognitive grasp. It follows that the experience of human value is beyond our control—a given, sovereign—even though our beliefs influence it.
- ✓ Existential reason builds on the sovereign subjectivity of human value and existence, which entails that induction is a valid method for gathering knowledge. So, we can apply the principles of rational thought to existential issues considered off-limits in the classical secular-dualistic paradigm. Existential reason is not intended to replace the scientific method but to complement it. It recognizes that all conceptual knowledge, even when logically deduced, mathematically proved, and empirically confirmed, is ultimately a belief and that we can use reason to ensure our beliefs are rational.

So, existential reason is about human value and how nondualistic thought can help create it. Nonduality involves that human value arises exclusively and unquestionably in subjective first-person experience. Hence, the individual ought to be the measure of all things in existential matters.

The False Promise of Mind Transcendence

Nothing is more human than the desire to escape our humanity. There are Harry Potter and superhero movies. Children pretend they are invisible and imagine moving objects with their minds. When we get older, we dream of staying young forever and operating quantum computers with sheer mind power. We envision angels and devils, eternal hunting fields and Valhalla, the fires of hell, and the miracle of reincarnation. And when we hope for a good outcome, we cross our fingers to summon benevolent forces.

Of course, rational people like me are immune to superstition. But when a black cat passes before me, I prefer a detour over crossing its path. And when I see a shooting star, I concentrate hard when I make my wish. I mean, you can never know, right?

The intense wish to find comfort beyond the uncertain human world fathers compelling thoughts. Our tiny and fragile presence in the universe's indifferent void almost forces us to conceive a just supernatural power we can rely on. In his 1975 book *The Tao of Physics*, Fritjof Capra wrote, "Science does not need mysticism and mysticism does not need science. But man needs both."

Although I was raised a Catholic, I lack sufficient knowledge of religions to comment on them. I find them fascinating, and my opinions about them aren't strong. I don't reject faith-based religions, but it seems fine to me when others do reject them—for themselves. However, telling others to do so as well seems ill-informed ethical advice. Nondualistic metaphysics implies that none of our concepts refers to anything real. So, to reject religions because God doesn't exist

4. THE NATURE OF OUR NONDUALITY

is hardly convincing. Nothing else we conceive exists either.

Some argue that religious beliefs promote individual and collective well-being and are, therefore, rational. However, opponents of faith-based religion point to the many examples where religious dogma interferes in worldly matters in abominable ways. Can we avoid a collision between rational thought and faith-based religion?

Rational nondualism solves this by applying a clean cut between the realms of rational thought (including science) and faith-based religion. Unknowable and mind-independent are tautological in our nondual world, so mind-independent knowledge is reserved for faith-based religion. Rational thought concerns mind-dependent knowledge.

This way, we respect Capra's view that science and mysticism don't need each other. Rational science remains clear of religious dogma, and religious people can get the respect they deserve because their faith in the supernatural doesn't overlap with rational science. It might not be easy in practice, but at least rational people could agree on these principles.

Religion and fiction invoke vivid images of the beyond-human, but our very own minds do so as well. When we try to understand the human mind, we shouldn't overlook the evolutionary processes that have shaped it. Evolution isn't particularly concerned with our well-being as individuals and a species because its goal is to achieve biological value beyond individual organisms and species. Evolution won't object if lizards or insects rule tomorrow's world.

Evolution has given us considerable mental capabilities, but they came at a price: the persistent inner conflict between our needs for the present and the future, for ourselves and others. We are suspended in a motivational force field between hope and fear, desire and responsibility, pride and shame, continuously challenging our wits.

Our mind is an excellent salesperson and promises the

world to get us to move our pretty backsides:[16]
- ✓ If you get this job, all your problems will be solved.
- ✓ If you are romantically involved with that person, you will be happy forever.

However, our mind tends to overpromise and underdeliver. After getting the job or being involved, the grass isn't always as green as it seemed. We still have our daily challenges and may find that our flame is quite a boring couch potato. "Don't worry," our mind tells us. "Here are a couple of new objectives for you to run after, and I promise you, this time, it will be different. You will have ended your suffering for good when you reach *these* goals. You'll be truly happy—and I mean forever!"

And so we go on and on, on the treadmill known as samsara. The promise of a conclusive end to our suffering is false because the human mind isn't made for eternal bliss. We have to live with our challenges and inner conflicts because they are part of being human.

Our mind doesn't only falsely promise that we can transcend our human limitations sentimentally but does so on a cognitive plain as well. It assures us that a table exists independently of our mind, meaning the mind can transcend into a mind-independent world. We have already unmasked this as a treacherous dualistic illusion. In science too, dualism gives rise to vain hopes of transcending our oneness with the world's intrinsically mysterious being:
- ✓ If we find the universe's ultimate physical law, we will have solved all mysteries.
- ✓ If we completely understand how our brain functions, we can solve all ethical issues.

In our highly advanced technological age, it is not popular

---

[16] Quite literally: the conscious mind of humans and other vertebrates comes with a peripheral motor nervous system and a high degree of mobility.

4. THE NATURE OF OUR NONDUALITY

to acknowledge that there are limits to what we can explain. History has often proved those pointing out such limitations wrong. However, everyone can verify that their subjective experience is intrinsically private. For example, we can never know if seeing the color blue is the same for any two persons. The privateness constitutes a technical limit to understanding the immediate conscious experience, making it a mystery.

The conscious mind cannot conceive and explain itself because it is inseparable from what it intends to conceive and explain. Once you truly understand that you *are* the mystery, it is no longer *required* to conceive or explain that mystery because you already fully know it—as *unconceived* knowledge. What more is there to know of what you already completely know? Nor is it necessary to *justify* your existence anymore. Since you are not separate from mysterious existence, to whom or what would you need to justify it? Instead, you may surrender to the mystery that you are and trust it to guide you.

Your mind chases its tail when it dualistically tries to wrap itself around the reality it is part of. Nondualism is marked by accepting mysterious existence without requiring an explanation or justification. Your being is truth itself, and you can use it to illuminate the conceptual worlds you imagine and find your way in them.

Evolution smiles approvingly and perhaps even slightly sardonically when your mind makes you forever chase mirages, always *just* out of reach. However, emboldened by nondualistic insight, you may defiantly tell evolution, "I am not your powerless puppet! *You* gave me my conscious mind, but *I* will darn well use it as I please!"

The enlightened mind stands out from the unenlightened by embracing that it cannot transcend itself. It speaks for itself that mind transcendence, be it emotionally, cognitively, or ethically, is a highly dualistic premise. Zen Buddhism depicts nirvana as freedom from samsara, but that freedom should not be conceived as an escape from it.

You are chained to samsara by your hope of escaping it. So,

you cannot find nirvana by searching. Nirvana has to find *you* and can only do so when you have emotionally and cognitively completely abandoned the idea of transcending the samsara of your human condition. The magic words are full surrender to the present, just as it is. You arrive at the gates of nirvana by accepting that you can't escape samsara—and truly feeling that you don't want to. Then, on the off chance, its bliss might find you in the present moment. So, my practical advice about nirvana is to forget about it.

Striving for mind transcendence is dualistic and a bad idea because it causes suffering. However, the transcendence concept is often used in spiritual practice and philosophy, for example, in *transcendental* meditation and Immanuel Kant's *transcendental* idealism and deduction. Surely, they know what they are doing? The devil is once again in the details: We need to understand the difference between mind transcendence and other types of transcendence.

For example, *self transcendence* seems a legitimate motivation to engage in spiritual practice. Self transcendence differs from mind transcendence in that the self is an illusion, but the conscious mind is not—it is our essence.

Transcendence to a higher consciousness, in which we let go of intrusive thoughts, is also a worthy cause. But when we conceive higher consciousness as an exalted spiritual world *separate* from our mind, it is not anymore—because that is dualistic.

Spiritual experiences can *transcend* the scope of common feelings. What I sensed when experimenting with zazen meditation was sensational. So, I can personally corroborate that such transcendence is possible. Many will also agree that psychoactive substances can open mind doors that usually remain shut. The fine line between nondualistic and dualistic transcendence is crossed, though, once the seeker or teacher considers it possible to exit the human mind altogether.

Transcendence in *philosophy* means exceeding the limits of

4. THE NATURE OF OUR NONDUALITY

human experience, which makes it necessarily dualistic. Typical Western philosophy is dualistic this way. It assumes there is a mind-independent truth and believes in our ability to transcend from our conscious experience into it. When scientists consider that measurements and the laws of physics reflect a mind-independent truth, they dualistically consider that we can temporarily check out of our mind world and pay a visit to the mystical dwellings of reality.

The duality and mind transcendence illusions are so pervasive that most consider the world nonsensical without them. For example, a consequence of nonduality is that we only have access to the present world. Some will protest, "How about history? Journalistic inquiry into yesterday's events? Aren't they explorations of worlds other than the present? Don't they show that we can transcend the present by going into the past?"

The rational answer must be *no*. History and yesterday's news are not transcendence into the past but present imagination. The past and the future may be factual but aren't real, and everything in the present with a meaning beyond the present isn't real either.

In summary, the human mind is exceedingly susceptible to the illusion of duality and the corresponding belief in mind transcendence. The very job of our mind is to imagine a mind-independent world, abound with carrots and sticks designed to spur our organism into action for its evolutionarily determined purposes. It is no small feat for that same mind to recognize that what it conceives, remembers, desires, and fears, even when highly relevant, isn't real beyond present experience. Facts are not reality.

As long as you don't see past the false promise of mind transcendence, you will remain more firmly in samsara's grip and easily deceived by promises of mind transcendence, even when such promises are well-intended.

Enlightenment is necessarily a subjective experience with an entirely personal meaning. We can only compare our experiences after conceiving them. Since enlightenment is pre-conceptual, words can only point to it. Spiritual teachers like Eckhart Tolle caution against reading too much into words—they are merely pointers to the nonduality, to be forgotten once we have found what we were looking for.

Indeed, enlightenment cannot be put into words. But the same holds for the smell of morning dew, the taste of fresh orange juice, or the feeling one gets when seeing the ocean: Instantaneous experience is always beyond words. Fortunately, that doesn't stop us from talking about it. It can be truly pleasant and helpful.

For example, a confusing choice of words can falsely give the impression that enlightenment is about mind transcendence. Eckhart Tolle teaches that the *mind* inhibits present awareness: Thinking too much about the past and the future distracts us from *the Now*.

While I fully agree with Tolle that thinking too much can get in the way of accessing, what he calls, *the power of Now*—a brilliant phrase—I prefer to conclude that, instead of the whole mind, *too much* thinking is an obstacle to being nondually aware. In my interpretation, the now *is* the mind. In terms of existence, the mind and the now have the same properties, so they are identical.

When you pay attention to what your first-person experience consists of, you will find that this experience is mind only and in nothing different from the present. Even your body translates into present feelings and perceptions. Nonduality means that you and I are nothing *but* mind, and so is the rest of the world. Our thoughts are part of that mind.

Perhaps the misunderstanding about "no mind" stems from something lost in translation. In Zen Buddhism, "mushin" is a state of consciousness reached by meditators and martial art practitioners who are free of thought and in harmony with the present flow. *Mushin* is often translated into English as simply "no-mind"—hence the misunderstanding—but it is worthwhile to note that mushin is the short form of "mushin no shin," a Zen expression meaning "the mind without mind." D.T. Suzuki translates mushin as "being free from mind-attachment."

Tolle's distinction between mind and awareness also doesn't match the neuroscientific terminology. Neuroscientists have precisely pinpointed the brain area responsible for sustaining awareness. Awareness is a low-detail wide-scope notion "in" the mind, just as a focused look at a flower is a high-detail narrow-scope notion. No meditation is needed to notice your ability to steer your *attention* from either something small in much detail or something large in not-so-much detail. You may focus your mind and senses on something like a lion on prey or pay attention to the amalgam of experiences, sensory and otherwise, in an altogether wide awareness of everything that's going on in the present. It would be a dualistic fallacy not to consider awareness part of the mind, regardless of your attention focus level.

Interestingly, neuroscience can also help us understand why we are highly susceptible to the illusion of duality. Neuroscientists have meticulously studied conscious short-term memory, which gets updated by *attention* with new sensory and long-term memory content, and found a rather scanty capacity of short-term memory that gets significantly enriched by long-term memory content. The predominance of long-term memory content in short-term memory breeds the illusion of duality: Our memories seem more real than the real present itself.

Several mindfulness meditation coaches teach to "widen" the attention during spiritual practice. For example, we are to observe that thoughts and feelings are like little clouds against a wide blue sky of awareness—and then, more and more, notice that who you really are, where the nonduality lies, is the wide blue sky of awareness.

While it is enthralling to meditate this way, the meditation coaches know that the "wide blue sky" is not yet the nonduality itself. It merely orients the mind toward it. Nondualistic metaphysics clarifies what is happening: It doesn't matter if we know something small in great detail or "wide and large" with "all senses open" in less detail; we are still *conceiving* in both cases. Whatever we conceive has to be a dualistic projection. Awareness is "simply" a notion of being alive, just like a color or a touch is a notion of seeing or feeling something. But awareness is not Tao. Tao is "simply" the feeling that equals being. If you recall, life and existence are not identical because life has meaning beyond the immediate present.

Tao is not identified by the width or breadth of what one conceives. The crucial difference between the conceptual world and the nonduality is that the former is conceived and the latter not.

Nonduality and Virtue

The lure of mind transcendence comes in assorted hard-to-resist flavors. Who hasn't ever dreamt of eternal youth? Lasting bliss? Or the revelation that solves the riddle of the universe? But also in ethics, the branch of knowledge dealing with moral principles, our ideas can be informed by our hopes and fancies.

We dream of a morally perfect society and like to idolize our examples. If only we could all be like Mother Theresa, Mahatma Gandhi, Martin Luther King Jr., or Nelson Mandela. Sometimes, we hope others are saintly and have lesser expectations of ourselves. Still, there is nothing more inspiring than courageous people fighting the good fight against the bad ones and standing up for the less fortunate.

4. THE NATURE OF OUR NONDUALITY

But Aleksandr Solzhenitsyn's 1973 *The Gulag Archipelago* reveals that the human mind is less perfect than our dreams. From the depths of human suffering caused by Stalinist oppression, he shows that the line between good and bad, between virtue and vice, doesn't run *between* people but through each and every one of us.[17] Solzhenitsyn describes how the utopian totalitarian Soviet state brings out the worst in people but also how some were able to cope due to their strength of character, perseverance, and a bit of luck.

Projecting absolute virtue on others or demanding it from ourselves is a typical byproduct of dualism. Virtue and vice are believed to be absolute and external to the human mind. Seemingly, envisioning a virtuous ideal only has advantages: Even when it is not reached, it will make people behave *more* virtuously, which benefits society.

But is absolute virtue philosophically possible? No! One only has to imagine having a deadly parasite living inside oneself to see that not all situations can be solved without losers. Few would object to taking the life of the deadly parasite to save their own. But even granting a mosquito a sip of one's blood is a sacrifice not many are willing to make. Who hasn't ever killed a mosquito? And is avoiding a little itch truly "objectively" more valuable than a mosquito's life? Would the mosquito agree with our ethical analysis? Also in less obvious human ethical issues, what is morally correct is often a matter of weighing interests, including one's own.

Paradoxically, upholding absolute virtue standards often leads to *less* virtuous behavior. By externalizing the moral truth, those who declare having access to it often allow themselves a

---

[17] Solzhenitsyn's famous quotes verbatim: "Gradually it was disclosed to me that the line separating good and evil passes not through states, nor between classes, nor between political parties either—but right through every human heart—and through all human hearts." And: "If only there were evil people somewhere insidiously committing evil deeds, and it were necessary only to separate them from the rest of us and destroy them. But the line dividing good and evil cuts through the heart of every human being. And who is willing to destroy a piece of his own heart?"

little more leeway than "the common people." After all, the burden of educating the hopelessly subjective masses merits compensation by privilege, right?

Secular dualism leads to double standards—and one only has to look at how those preaching carbon dioxide emission reductions are hopping around the world in their private jets to see it in all its ugliness, undermining society's motivation to deal with the urgent climate change problem. It's also telling how many white middle-aged male leaders, in the name of inclusivity and diversity, call for fewer white middle-aged males in charge in their organizations while categorically refusing to cede their own position—higher than anyone's so with the greatest potential impact on inclusivity.

One can only justify doling out moral rules one isn't ready to follow oneself if one dualistically feels above the public. Double standards in egalitarian societies breach the rational law of non-contradiction. From a nondualistic viewpoint, a leader or celebrity should practice the virtue they preach to remain credible. In dualistic societies, leaders lead by moralizing, in free nondualistic ones, by example.

The essential issues of inclusivity and diversity deserve better than hypocritical moralizing. A more rational approach involves a meaningful and unequivocal definition of these words and a practical understanding of what tomorrow's inclusive and diverse organization should look like. What is the purpose? Empowerment or dependency? Inclusion or division? Equity or a photo op? Fair and sensible minds apply the principles of rational thought when they endeavor for inclusivity:

- ✓ They respect the law of non-contradiction. They don't fight racism and sexism by stigmatizing and scapegoating white males.
- ✓ They respect the law of identity of indiscernibles. They don't consider demonizing and canceling people based on their beliefs an expression of compassion and tolerance.
- ✓ They respect the law of the excluded middle. They don't

4. THE NATURE OF OUR NONDUALITY

change the meaning of phrases like *the presumption of innocence, fair trial, respect for the individual*, and *inclusiveness* depending on whom they apply it to.
✓ They respect the principle of sufficient reason. They don't call for divisive measures to achieve more unity.

Existential reason can be applied to matters of morality, in our secular-dualistic day and age too often considered off-limits for rational discussion or entirely the territory of experts.

Nondualistic metaphysics entails that virtue isn't absolute. Ethics is a typical existential matter, and although expert opinion and scientific analysis are invaluable, the ultimate answer is *not* determined by expertise and empirical science. Instead, it is a matter of our hearts and minds. Existential reason helps us to have fair and solution-driven discussions about them.

❋

Vegetarians and vegans don't eat animals. In addition to not consuming animal flesh, vegans don't consume milk products, eggs, honey, or any other product derived from an animal.[18] In my humble opinion, both are perfectly legitimate stances. I don't want to change anyone's diet. Instead, I bring them up because analyzing people's motives for such lifestyle choices helps us understand the difference between dualistic and nondualistic ethics. I will first discuss these types of ethics before applying them to vegetarianism and veganism.

Dualistic metaphysics comes in many shapes and forms. Religious dualism envisions a divine truth above, so separate from the human realms. Vegetarianism, veganism, and other modes of living can be based on such views. I admit my

---
[18] According to the PETA website www.peta.org/living/food/whats-the-difference-between-vegetarian-and-vegan/. Retrieved in May 2023.

ignorance of these religious motives, so I will spare you my comments. Rather, I speak here of another kind of dualism: of those who believe in a knowable reality and spread the gospel of objective knowledge. They envision a mind-independent truth as the touchstone of truthful human knowledge. Their faith in the human intellect and technology is so steadfast that they trust the mind to do the impossible: penetrate a super-human, sovereign, mind-independent world beyond itself.

It is hard for the human mind to shake the belief in supernatural entities. This belief is so deeply ingrained that it goes unnoticed by many holding it. Even people at the apex of intelligence, including Einstein, suppose that truth is independent of the human mind.

In secular dualism, reality decides what is objectively true or not. From that position, it is a small step to believe that reality also judges right and wrong human behavior. In dualistic ethics, virtue and vice are independent of the human mind. They are absolute.

So, dualistic ethics leads to the uncomfortable situation that all guilt feelings require absolution from a super-human judge of right and wrong. In a dualistic setting, for every wrong action, there is a right one, ignoring the philosophical and psychological observation that human needs cannot ever be entirely conflict-free. And in secular dualism, Jesus did not die on the cross for our sins, so we are forever sinners and never off the hook.

Since *all* conceived knowledge breaches the oneness of being, secular dualists must consider *all* their thoughts "unconsciously biased." Intelligent, sincerely egalitarian secular dualists cannot tolerate guilt because their worldview makes guilt and self-worth logically incompatible.[19] They have no cognitive recourse when accusers point out their role in the world's woes—merely not doing something about it enough to

---

[19] Paradoxically, relatively intelligent secular dualists may be more acutely aware of the irreconcilability of guilt with their worldview, hence more prone to moralizing, scapegoating, and, inevitably, hypocrisy.

4. THE NATURE OF OUR NONDUALITY

be blameworthy.

If one wants to understand the present-day Western victimhood cult, one merely needs to analyze secular dualism. Secular dualism offers a pedestal to victimhood and leads to oikophobia[20] because the *subjective*, first-person "we"—however defined: by ethnicity, religion, sexual orientation, culture, or even species—are intrinsically guilty for merely existing and less worthy than the *objective*, third-person "others."

Do you ever wonder why in the West, an elite could rise to power that preaches tolerance toward all religions except for Christianity and that, in the name of anti-racism, considers white people liable for the privilege of the skin color they were born with? Secular dualism's irrationality is your answer. In contrast, existential reason is less about identity politics and more about freedom of religion, true color-blindness, and equal opportunity because it recognizes the individual as the nondual source of human value.

In nondualistic ethics, there are still right and wrong actions. Nondualists are not impervious to moral imperatives, remorse, indebtedness, honor, admiration, and gratitude. However, these feelings are not absolute. They can be understood as psychological phenomena with over a century-old Darwinian and Freudian explanations.

Evolution didn't endow us with *negatives* like guilt, fear, pain, and aggression to gleefully torment us, but for its Darwinian biological purposes. Every quality of our body and mind has survived the ages, so assuming they aren't evolutionarily determined would be unreasonable. But these natural negatives, although designed to create *biological* value, are often not propitious to creating *human* value. Fortunately, evolution has also endowed us with intelligence which we can use to pursue human value instead of merely heeding evolution's

---

[20] Oikophobia is fear of the familiar, as opposed to xenophobia which is fear of the unfamiliar. Oikophobes tend to be overly critical of their own culture and ethnicity, while xenophobes are overly critical of other cultures and ethnicities.

more primitive calls.

Evolution spurs the human intellect with feelings like pride and shame, hope and fear. Unlike dualistic ethics, which considers the human species separate from animal species because of our intellectual capabilities, nondualistic ethics accepts that the human species, although intelligent, is nonetheless "just" another species. Considering humans a world apart from nature and other species is flattering but not entirely rational.

In nondualistic ethics, if one does the right thing, one doesn't seek extramundane approval but ultimately wishes to please oneself. The nondualist modestly admits ignorance of otherworldly preferences. Altruism must have its roots in self-interest because it can only result from the altruist's mind. Guilt feelings are uncomfortable and painful. With good feelings, evolution rewards virtue; with bad feelings, it taxes vice.

Do avowed nondualists, who reject absolute ethical rules, live less virtuously than secular dualists? Probably rather the opposite: One only needs to look at the integrity and kindness of Buddhist monks to see that nondualism leads to virtue rather than vice.

Vegetarianism can be based on dualistic and nondualistic ethical views. A vegetarian nondualist may feel bad for the animals and not want to bear responsibility for killing them by eating their meat. A vegan nondualist might consider that getting cows pregnant and stealing their calves just for them to produce milk is cruel, as is stealing eggs from chickens so that they keep on producing new ones. But nondualists may be more aware than dualists that guilt is an inescapable human condition.[21] The nondualist might weigh up ethical considerations and be more tolerant of a certain level of guilt.

For a nondualist, there is no contradiction in being vegetarian but not vegan because we are inseparable from

---

[21] In terms of Jungian psychology, they may have better "integrated their shadow."

4. THE NATURE OF OUR NONDUALITY

nature as members of the human species. No absolute ethical law keeps us from eating honey and eggs. Not doing so is ultimately a personal consideration of how guilty it makes one feel and how much guilt one is willing to bear.

However, a *dualistic* vegetarian who is not vegan has to deal with a serious cognitive discrepancy: How can one reject eating animals but accept exploiting them? More generally speaking, how can one have *any* guilt feeling and continue living as one does? Rigorous secular-dualistic ethics is logically incompatible with guilt feelings because they signal failure relative to an absolute virtue standard.

The resulting cognitive dissonance can be so forceful that it turns the dualist into a moralist who externalizes all guilt and projects it on others. Dualists may zealously endeavor to change other people's culinary customs.

To remain consistent with their irrational dualism, such moralists often see humanity as an intruder in pristine nature. They consider us a pest and become anti-human. The only logically consistent option (which I don't recommend!) from this irrational perspective is—I'm sorry to say—suicide. Fortunately, some primordial fear keeps most secular dualists from this ultimate act of objectivity. However, as a substitute, they may resort to scapegoating lest they lose their illusion of purity and moral excellence. The secular dualists' only hope for redemption is *cancellation*—but preferably of others than themselves. In Freudian psychology, this unconscious defense mechanism is known as projection.

Dualists, in their certitude of being closer to the objective truth than others, may always consider themselves external to ethical issues. They might feel that moralizing and chastising others absolves them of their guilt.

As you may remember from *Chapter 2*, another typical secular dualism issue is that it entails that free will is an illusion. In a dualistic paradigm, the physical brain reality deterministically causes the mind, so the perception of free will in that mind must be an illusion. Without free will, there cannot be *sin* either,[22] so there is no justification for punishing criminals except for rehabilitation purposes.

Many legal experts in my native country, the Netherlands, argue that offenders should not receive more punishment than what is known to reduce the probability of recidivism. They see the criminal justice system predominantly as a training tool for innocent but uneducated minds on their way back to the right path. When lenient sentences for ghastly crimes cause uproar in Dutch society, ironically, these dualistic experts tend to chide the public for their *irrational* and primitive ("populistic") tendencies.

In contrast, a nondualistic worldview implies that free will is not an illusion but an essence. So, while rehabilitation is indeed a central task of criminal justice systems, it is not the only one. Its purpose (besides protecting society) is also reasonable reprisal since it substitutes private retribution and vigilantism. The law of non-contradiction forbids considering sentences fair if they systematically and flagrantly violate society's sense of justice.[23]

Nondualism compels people to shoulder their guilt. The actors in lawmaking and criminal justice are liable to society, the victims of crime, and the principles of rational thought.

The next subchapter deals with other existential issues illustrating existential reason's vigor. I am not external to our nondual world, so I approach them from my point of view. Reason invites holders of divergent opinions to dialogue. I don't mind learning rational counterarguments.

---

[22] The attentive reader might notice that secular dualism leads to both the impossibility of sin *and* the inescapability of guilt feelings. This perplexing contradiction is yet another sign of secular dualism's philosophical inaccuracy.
[23] To be clear, nondualism and existential reason do not require a change of legal standards and suspects' entitlement to comprehensive legal protection.

4. THE NATURE OF OUR NONDUALITY

THE WAY OF OUR NONDUAL HEARTS

Nondualism is scary. Without the certainty of religion or the outside world's existence, we are confronted with deep-rooted fears of emptiness, loneliness, and helplessness.

But the price of secular dualism is also high. Positing a higher truth leaves us guilty of not always being equanimous, innocent, perfect, and right. When we are not, we have failed compared to an external higher standard. We aren't sufficiently *mindful*, virtuous, and knowledgeable.

Dualism also burdens us with discovering who we are and finding our purpose in life because there must be a reason why we were put on the planet. It is up to ourselves to find out why. Nothing can mitigate our absolute guilt in secular dualism: no Savior, carnival, confession, or reasonable limits.

When the mind awakens to nondual existence, it relinquishes all certainty it thought it could find in the dualistic conceptual worlds. The mind arrives in the now and lets go of yesterday and tomorrow. It takes courage to allow your mind to do just that. Such courage can only be found when the mind is certain of its conclusion that the conceptual worlds aren't real. It takes courage to accept the mystery—that it is okay that we don't know who we are and why we are here. But the freedom one gains is immeasurable.

- ✓ Your well-being is no longer primarily determined by external factors.
- ✓ Your access to inner truth makes your opinions matter—particularly when they are rational.

Enlightenment dramatically increases your sovereignty over well-being and truth. This doesn't mean you can choose what is true because Tao's truth is beyond your control. Instead, it means that you are not *separate* from Tao's sovereign truth emerging instantaneously in you.

In our secular-dualistic Western society, we are still

cognitively disconnected from subjectivity and pay a high price for that, individually and collectively. Existential reason can remedy this: As a subjective but rational way of thinking, existential reason acknowledges that truth and human value transpire exclusively and spontaneously in the individual and seeks to incorporate this nondualistic fact into our way of life. Existential reason connects the mind with the heart.

Secular dualism, with its irrational faith in our ability to transcend our humanity, projects *perfection* in your mind: perfect objectivity, perfect happiness, perfect beauty, perfect conduct. Once you grasp the nonduality of your existence, you can learn instead to let your nondual heart (Tao) be your guiding star. This can help you to worry less. You will be more mentally present, natural, in touch with your feelings, and appreciative of imperfections. Broadly speaking:

- ✓ Tao gives you autonomy over your inner peace because it is literally the answer to all your problems.
- ✓ Tao makes you naturally assertive because it helps you trust your feelings and act accordingly.

In other words, Tao makes you calm, confident, and assertive. Does that perhaps sound familiar—especially to dog lovers? The question of how to live in the moment is certainly not the exclusive domain of philosophers, spiritual seekers, and curious engineers. In his YouTube show *Dog Nation*, the famous *dog whisperer* César Millán explains how dogs can feel when you aren't mentally present and act out to fill the void. I am a big César fan. He teaches how dogs help their masters become better persons.

Dogs are experts at living in the now and will let you know when you don't. According to Millán, there's nothing wrong with thinking, but you shouldn't forget to feel. The key is confidence: calm and assertive energy. Confidence allows you to be presently aware and spontaneous because you don't think too much about yesterday and tomorrow.

Millán's advice also applies beyond the relationship between dogs and their masters. Not all your thoughts are a threat to

4. THE NATURE OF OUR NONDUALITY

your mindfulness and spiritual well-being. Your present musings are inseparable from your nondual existence. So, the question is not how to stop thinking but how to be sufficiently confident in life so you don't get lost in your thoughts.

Tao can give you such confidence.

While we are on *mindfulness*, fathoming nondualistic metaphysics can help spiritual seekers avoid pitfalls when they aspire to this state of mind. Spiritual practice, like meditation, is often about *emptying* the mind. So, what should we make of the term mind*ful*ness?

In secular-dualistic thinking, all human meaning is thought to reside in the conceptual world. So, to enjoy the present moment to the fullest, we need to "suck it all in" and be supremely aware of all the joys that befall us. In this way, *mindfulness* is perhaps typically Western dualistic terminology.

The nondualistic worldview clarifies what "mind-empty" meditation is all about: Since all meaning and value reside in unconceived experience rather than the conceptual world, the meditator merely has to stop generating concepts to be in touch with the value and truth of undivided being. The less we try to hold on to concepts, the more we are presently aware and free to marvel at Tao's splendor for its own sake.

Since Tao is so fundamental, there are countless other ways in which it can promote your personal well-being. Once you *get* nondualism, you will find them and recognize them in the work of spiritual teachers. One more personal example: I struggled with *ruminating* until I found Tao. I find it difficult to stop thinking and relax. I used to overthink life decisions and could never make up my mind. I felt that as long as I had doubts, I had to think just a little harder to find the right solution.

My wonderful family and friends recommended to listen to my feelings instead of thinking too much. But it wasn't until I found Tao that I deeply understood *why* the answer to all questions is in our hearts instead of cognition: The imagined conceptual worlds can't be perfect, but our nondual hearts can't go wrong. Ever since, I have stopped overthinking.

This doesn't mean I never wake up at 4 a.m. anymore with a racing mind. But that's okay. That's just how I am. Tao also lets me be at peace with it.

※

When we broaden our view from individual to collective existential issues, we find that secular dualism causes similar problems on a larger scale. Due to our insistence on value-free objective knowledge, secular-dualistic Western cultures may lack calm and assertive energy akin to secular-dualistic individuals. The disconnectedness from our subjectivity can leave us rudderless, nervous, and timid.

With reason out of the picture, Western thought categorizes societal existential issues as scientifically meaningless or merely matters of personal preference, expertise, fashion, or discourse. This is a fundamental mistake. The truth doesn't exist independently from our minds, but that doesn't mean it isn't factual. Nondualism beckons us beyond conceived knowledge to find it—in unconceived knowledge.

For all the good that empirical science and technological progress have brought us, the Western world has reached an impasse because its dualistic answers to existential matters are inadequate. Let me ask you this: Do you consider that the Western world is currently awake or asleep? I contend that we are in a deep slumber and that our lack of trust in reason to cope with existential issues is largely to blame.

As an admittedly naive engineer, I see a Western world that is becoming *less* rational. Perhaps paradoxically, secularization is partly to blame. Before the twentieth century, the West was mostly Christian. Religious dualism since, give or take, the fourteenth century gave reason enough leeway to allow for the Renaissance, Enlightenment, and incredible scientific and technological progress to happen. Reason could coexist with religion because the former dealt with worldly affairs while the

4. THE NATURE OF OUR NONDUALITY

latter focused more on pious matters.

The twentieth century was one of secularization, yet the West remained firmly dualistic. We could argue that the supreme being of God was replaced by a new deity: *reality* or the mind-independent truth. We have already established that the belief in human access to reality rests on a compelling illusion. Reality and God have in common that people without miraculous extrasensory abilities must confess they cannot know them. If they talk about them anyway, they do so on faith-based, religious grounds.

More than God, divine reality is a busybody who loves to meddle in worldly affairs. In secular dualism, reason and empiricism compete for knowledge of reality and are largely incompatible. The irrational belief in an external truth erodes the trust in reason in favor of empiricism because reason is not the product of "reality" but of "the mind." This is why secular dualism is potentially less rational than religious dualism.[24]

As secular dualism leads individuals to perfectionism, so does it lead societies to *utopianism* because it implies that there is a perfect way of doing things. The twentieth century was indeed marred by utopian ideologies like nazism and communism that led to immeasurable suffering.

At the end of the twentieth century, communism collapsed. Western thinkers like Francis Fukuyama, who was perhaps even more naive than I, prophesied that this was "the end of history."[25] He predicted the universalization of Western liberal democracy as the final form of human government and the end-point of humankind's ideological evolution. Western liberal democracy was Fukuyama's utopia, and he was convinced that societies would automatically gravitate toward it.

---

[24] Secular and religious dualism are both less rational than nondualism because only a nondualistic paradigm requires neither a supernatural assumption nor a contradiction between reason and empiricism. Nondualism acknowledges that no knowledge is without a subject, so all knowledge is ultimately empirical.

[25] Francis Fukuyama (1992), *The End of History and the Last Man*.

Partly in response to Fukuyama, Samuel P. Huntington made a harsher prediction in his 1996 book *The Clash of Civilizations and the Remaking of World Order*: New conflicts would arise between the West and other civilizations. Huntington didn't advocate conflicts but used historical analysis to present a descriptive hypothesis. It seems that Huntington's more rational, less utopian prediction has proved more accurate and that it is to the West's detriment that we didn't heed his warnings. Huntington applied the rational principle of sufficient reason, while Fukuyama resorted to wishful thinking.

Today's Western secular dualism leads to harmful utopianism and overly reliance on empirical evidence at the expense of reason. Hume's problem of induction echoes loudly across Western parliaments, where politicians are judged on their good intentions rather than rational problem-solving and planning.

A rational engineer solving a problem analyzes situation A, defines the desired situation B in sufficient detail, and then practically plans the steps from A to B. But calls for such practicality fall flat when politicians insist on empirical proof of predicted results, which is, of course, only available after the fact. Instead, they often prefer short-term symbolic actions and whipping up fears and other emotions.

Politicians may unjustly use the problem of induction as an excuse for irrational decisions and power politics. A democratic society that demands respect for the principles of rational thought is less inclined to utopian, demagogic, and harmful government.

For example, the crucial climate change issue suffers from a lack of rationality. I don't deny the extraordinary progress made in fighting it, and I am grateful to the many who are working so hard to get it right. I merely suggest that we have room for improvement by becoming more rational. Instead of relying on fear, we should turn to hope. Instead of apocalyptic

4. THE NATURE OF OUR NONDUALITY

prophecies, we must make rational plans.

Much of the irrational moralizing, hypocrisy, and doomsaying surrounding climate change is counterproductive and seems to emanate from a secular-dualistic understanding of the world. Whenever humankind has risen to the occasion, it has always been through reason, compassion, and courage. Solving climate change starts by accepting that we are one with nature and, as a species, have legitimate needs. Only if we accept our humanity and every individual's responsibility can we come together to solve this problem—with reason.

Since I take the climate change issue at heart, let's apply existential reason to the actions of protest groups like Extinction Rebellion and Last Generation. They seek to reduce carbon dioxide emissions through behavior change by blocking busy roads in Western countries. Their deepest convictions are revealed by their words to the upset drivers they dupe: "We are here for you and your children too." In other words, they are convinced they are helping people and their families with their actions. *Reason* allows us to analyze these actions, *existential reason* to judge them.

- ✓ Do the activists apply the law of non-contradiction?
  Do they realize that it is irrational to help people by obstructing them?
- ✓ Do they apply the law of the excluded middle?
  Is their understanding of the concept of helping people meaningful and coherent? Do they acknowledge that in democratic societies that allow protest, the individual has the primacy over how they wish to be helped?
- ✓ Do they apply the law of identity of indiscernibles?
  If their definition of helping other people shares all properties with helping themselves feel more virtuous, shouldn't we conclude that they are only helping themselves?
- ✓ Do they apply the principle of sufficient reason?
  Do they consider the risk that their divisive actions will *erode* the support for decisive climate actions and lead to

more carbon dioxide emissions?

In a typical secular-dualistic manner, these performative activists believe themselves closer to the "objective truth" than the rest of us because they consider themselves better informed and probably more pure, virtuous, and intelligent. This absolute certainty allows them to cruelly stop sick people from going to the hospital and nurses and teachers from going to work.

Secular dualism tends to incentivize and justify inhumane behavior because what is right and virtuous is considered above what is humane. The activists claim the world's end is near, so their acts are a desperate last resort. But is their desperation warranted by the facts and thereby acceptable? Do they clearly understand how their actions will save the world from annihilation? Existential reason demands that the authorities require better justifications for these thoroughly premediated, noxious actions than mere irrational fear before sympathizing with the activists' intentions and considering leniency.

It must come as no surprise that the same activist groups, in the name of the objective higher truth, also target our defenseless cultural heritage in museums in ways that echo what the Taliban did to the Buddhas of Bamiyan and ISIS in Palmyra. Last century's communism and nazism remind us that, if unchecked, there is no limit to inhumanity in the name of supreme revelations. Like end-of-history prophecies, end-of-the-world prophecies have accompanied humanity since its inception, have never come true, and have never solved any problem.

Another presently hotly debated collective existential issue is gender definition. I consider myself a liberal, felt exceedingly at home living in free-spirited Amsterdam, and have friends dealing with questions about their gender. This is to show that I am not prejudiced and have an open mind. I intend to demonstrate that existential reason approaches this issue in

4. THE NATURE OF OUR NONDUALITY

ways that respect the dignity of all involved.

A quick search on the internet shows that our secular-dualistic society currently estimates the number of human genders as anywhere between two and seventy-two. For every list of genders, forceful arguments are brought to bear.

The proponents of recognizing more genders point out that the traditional two biological genders are subjective social constructs. They use this—in their view—groundbreaking discovery to argue for recognizing more than two genders: Many people subjectively identify differently from being a woman or a man and are being victimized by society's constructs. So, experts on this side of the issue may consider it more "objective" to include in their list and tally all genders they find people subjectively identifying as.

Nonduality, however, leads to the realization that even the traditional two genders don't *exist* since they are merely conceptual. So, the correct number of existing genders is . . . zero! Indeed, the genders woman and man are social constructs, but so are literally all other concepts words refer to. Language doesn't reflect an objective reality but a culture's desire to communicate.

So, the genders our societies wish to recognize are primarily a matter of historic and organic cultural development instead of expert revelation. Everyone is free to use the words of their choosing to refer to whichever concepts they want, including their gender. But others use language too. Language loses its communication function if communities are no longer allowed to build consensus on vocabulary and how to use it. Many languages, like Spanish and French, are entirely built around the distinction between the traditional two genders.

In classical secular-dualistic fashion, the "more genders" proponents may feel closer to the "objective truth" than others. They project their guilt onto others by gender-word-policing and moralizing them to consider victims' feelings. But nondualistic light on the same actions exposes tyranny because they impose a minority view that undermines our societies' ability to communicate, coexist, and cooperate.

Secular dualists may dream of preserving their innocence by always staying on the right side of an absolute ethical standard. But nonduality implies that such a standard isn't possible. No one can remain without sin, and there is no gender definition without drawbacks.

It is not at all up to me which genders we should recognize in the future. But the nondualistic realization that there is no objective truth generally invites more democracy as the answers to collective existential issues are no longer a matter of expertise alone. Existential reason points to people's hearts and minds for solving issues beyond empirical science.

※

Western secular dualists, philosophically prone to seeing free will as an illusion, may be less concerned with individual freedom than rational nondualists. They are more likely to consider that "objective" supranational institutions—and their national counterparts—should have the prerogative to curb liberties when dealing with global issues like climate change, pandemics, and terrorism. They put more trust in objective policy than in the subjective individual.

Undoubtedly, our global challenges require extensive global coordination. But how far should we go in relinquishing freedom on their behalf? Rational nondualism implies that the individual is the measure of all things since it is where human value is "produced." This entails that collective existential issues should not be dealt with on a higher level than necessary—ensuring maximum individual freedom.

If we, for the sake of argument, subdivide the world into one camp for less freedom and another for more freedom, we find the secular dualists in the former and the rational nondualists in the latter. Worldwide, the less-freedom camp is more crowded than the more-freedom camp: There are more autocratic than democratic societies—and even within democratic societies, there are many undemocratic forces.

History has shown that vibrant democratic societies foster innovation and a robust middle class. But autocratic actors may see them as a threat and point their arrows at the Achilles heel of free societies: the "truth pillars" of knowledge and justice. Free societies collapse without their *truth pillars*, vindicating the less-freedom camp. Raw power then prevails over truth.

Freedom's foes encounter relatively little opposition from the utopian secular dualists, who have no cognitive recourse when inconspicuous attacks on the *truth pillars* are packaged as "objective" actions. In contrast, rational nondualists don't require necessary reasons but merely sufficient reasons to defend truth and freedom. This dramatically increases our potential for critical thought. It makes us more proactive and assertive. For example, it invites the public to hold the *truth pillar* actors accountable to the principles of rational thought, making them less susceptible to subversion and incompetence. We are no longer condemned to wait until irrational and harmful policies show their devastating empirical effects.

The facts surrounding the COVID-19 pandemic illustrate that this is more than just an academic discussion. When I write this, the outbreak started over three years ago. In the meantime, the number of casualties is six million and counting. However, the Western *truth pillars* have been remarkably reluctant and slow to recognize what was all over the internet since early 2020 and corroborated by scientific papers: that bat viruses with human HIV and SARS insertions don't evolve naturally. The principles of rational thought and our trust are breached in equal measure. We still don't know why such catastrophes happen and how they can be avoided.

Existential reason emancipates "outsider" citizens of the global village like me to ask questions even without knowing "all the facts" merely for being a human participant in existence. As Banksy isn't known by all his facts, so doesn't the smell of funny business announce itself merely by "all the facts." One doesn't need to be an expert to notice incoherences, contradictions, and patterns that justify rational questions—the type of questions curious engineers and principled journalists like.

Einstein developed his entire general relativity theory from a *single* data point: that the speed of light is independent of its direction and the Earth's relative motion. We should learn from Einstein. In our secular dualism, with its emphasis on empirical proof at the expense of reason, we often forget to *think* while foolishly waiting for the "proof in reality."

All human value emerges beyond our conceptual understanding in the Tao of every one of us. Our biggest mistake is considering subjectivity insignificant because we cannot explain it. From Chinese Taoist philosophy, we can learn that secular dualism is irrational. It leaves the West vulnerable to determined actors who *are* in touch with their subjective interests.

We can draw more wisdom from China's astounding cultural heritage, like Sun Tzu's *The Art of War*: "If you know the enemy and know yourself, you need not fear the result of a hundred battles. If you know yourself but not the enemy, for every victory gained, you will also suffer a defeat. If you know neither the enemy nor yourself, you will succumb in every battle."

By externalizing the truth, the West has inadvertently delegated the right to plea for its interests to the "objective" actors. Our belief in reason is our strength, but our belief in immaculate, value-free objective knowledge our weakness. Rational nondualism emancipates the Western mind from the sway of the imaginary beyond-human and validates its natural feelings of truth, justice, and morality.

Nondualism and reason are also potent antidotes to the irrational Western arrogance and misguided pretense of being the keepers of the objective truth. The West doesn't have to be a threat to the rest of the world if it knows its place shoulder-to-shoulder with the others instead of above them and stops meddling in the name of objectivity.

The West needs Chinese wisdom, but ultimately, China also needs the West to stand its ground because Western freedom brings innovation to the world. The West can only be assertive if it understands the inevitability end legitimacy of its subjective needs, notwithstanding our shared rational goals of peace and a fair, unbiased, and compassionate world. The rest of the world needs more Western perspicacity and confidence because it requires a global partner it can respect and lean on.

Nondualistic philosophy concerns mind-dependent issues and leaves room for cultural differences and mind-independent religious beliefs. Accordingly, nondualism is the basis for mutual respect, worldwide cooperation, modesty in the face of our challenges, and reason as a common ground.

※

Many in the West are blissfully unaware of the storm that is brewing. Others see dark clouds gathering and are understandably exasperated by the events unfolding under their very eyes. For example, only a decade ago, authors like George Orwell, Aldous Huxley, and H.G. Wells stood for vision and literary bravery in the face of tyranny. Today, a British government agency red-flags them as potentially "radicalizing influences." Freedom is under siege, and many feel helpless as Orwell's and Kafka's monitions come true, one by one.

Perhaps not unsurprisingly, the ancient Greek philosophy of Stoicism is making a comeback against this ominous backdrop. Stoicism is a philosophy that originated in ancient Greece and was later developed in ancient Rome. Stoics believe people should focus on what they can control in life and not worry about what they cannot control. They advocate a sense of detachment from external circumstances and a focus on inner experience instead. Stoicism teaches that the path to happiness and peace of mind is through developing self-control and living in accordance with reason and virtue.

Although detachment and reason are nondualistic principles, Stoicism isn't a nondualistic philosophy at all. It envisions *logos* as a higher truth: a divine order ("cosmic reason") that governs the universe for the good of all. Stoics are supposed to use reason and be virtuous to align themselves with logos and achieve inner peace. Stoics understand reason as what makes us human as opposed to our animalistic emotional side.

In other words, Stoics dualistically hope to transcend their minds to achieve inner peace. The Stoic nirvana is freedom of the passions. As in any explicitly or implicitly dualistic philosophy, such dualism leads to cognitive issues. Since Stoics seek inner peace by being virtuous and passion free, they enthusiastically label everything that is not virtue or vice as "indifferents." Their self-control allows them to be in harmony and peace without their fulfillment. Health, comfort, recognition, beauty, pleasure: the Stoic denies their importance. Yet, some indifferents are less indifferent than others, which is why they distinguish preferred indifferents from dispreferred indifferents: a contradiction in terms that shows that Stoics are human after all.

Whereas Stoicism isn't an explicitly dualistic philosophy but has dualistic principles, Epicureanism isn't an explicitly nondualistic philosophy, yet based on the nondualistic premise of categorically accepting our humanity. The philosophy focuses on achieving happiness and peace of mind through the pursuit of pleasure and avoidance of pain, with an emphasis on simple pleasures such as friendship, intellectual pursuits, and the enjoyment of nature.

Epicureanism teaches that pleasure and pain are the ultimate criteria for evaluating any action or thing, and that

4. THE NATURE OF OUR NONDUALITY

pleasure can be obtained through the satisfaction of natural and necessary desires, such as the desire for food, shelter, and companionship. Epicureans hold that excessive or artificial desires, such as the desire for wealth or power, are ultimately harmful and to be avoided. In nondualism, pleasure and pain are not different from human value. Human value arises instantaneously and spontaneously, so undeniably, from our nondual hearts.

Like Stoicism, Epicureanism also emphasizes cultivating a sense of detachment from external circumstances by focusing on inner tranquility. Epicureans believe that fear of death and the gods are among the greatest sources of anxiety. Individuals can achieve inner peace and contentment by recognizing and accepting the natural limits of human existence. Sounds familiar? No wonder Epicurus and Lao Tzu could get along so well!

To wrap it up, both Stoics and Epicureans believe in reason and hope for inner peace, but Stoicism is rooted in virtue, as opposed to Epicureanism in human value. I believe no one would deny the Stoics their virtuous sense of responsibility. However, Epicureanism's roots in humanity make it a more natural way of living. Instead of chaining our hearts, limiting them, it suggests awaking our hearts and listening carefully to them.

We don't have to feel guilty for our needs and desires. Our existence is a marvelous mystery, and we are free to use our minds to make the best of it. We can follow our inner truth and trust our being, just as it is.

COMMON OBJECTIONS TO NONDUALISM

I noticed that nondualism and existential reason invoke a host of knee-jerk reactions. Many people are curious about nondualism, but still relatively few willing to consider it. You may get similar reactions if you want to talk about it. Here are several, including my comments.

"Existential reason is too cerebral. People aren't always rational. Nonduality should be about spirituality and feeling instead of thinking."

Existential reason corrects irrational dualistic beliefs to allow for enlightenment. Once the nonduality is grasped, it is indeed unnecessary to keep thinking about it. One can stay in touch with the Tao by feeling. This gives the confidence to overthink less in daily life.

"Nondualism means that the truth doesn't exist independently from the mind. This makes the truth subjective, which means the end of science and justice."

In nondualism, the undivided truth known as Tao is not merely subjective because it unites the subject and object. Nondualism implies that truth is not a choice. If truth were a choice, we wouldn't be able to tell lies because we could choose our beliefs. So, our ability to tell lies shows that truth is factual even though it isn't mind-independent. Hence, truth remains the solid foundation of rational science and justice. Nondualism and existential reason imply neither a change in the scientific method nor in legal standards.

"The ultimate objective truth and ethical standard may not be achievable, but we need to posit it anyway to encourage fairness, virtuous behavior, and peace."

It is entirely existential-rational to avoid bias in order to promote trust, cooperation, and peace. The difference between ultimate impartiality and objectivity is that the former takes all people into account and the latter none. Nondualism entails that we have no choice but to trust our humanity and that society's *truth pillars* can be held to the standard of rational thought. Knowledge and ethical standards needn't be mind-independent for societies to thrive.

4. THE NATURE OF OUR NONDUALITY

"Nondualism is speculative. We should only take knowledge that we can verify (in reality) seriously."

... And how do we verify that statement? To call rational nondualism speculative and irrational dualism verifiable is self-defeating dogmatism. Dualism implies speculation about a supernatural mind-reality connection. As long as we ignore the plentiful facts that vindicate nonduality, the West will continue its slide on the slippery slope of irrationality.

"It is unscientific to claim that consciousness cannot be conceptually explained. History has always proved science and technology skeptics wrong, and the rapid progress in artificial intelligence (AI) shows that we are close to understanding and building artificial consciousness."

Real consciousness (Tao) is unconceived knowledge, private, and not just an attribute but our essence. Accordingly, our consciousness cannot conceptually explain itself because it cannot lift itself by the bootstraps. Since we can't conceive consciousness, we can't artificially build it either. No matter how intelligent, AI without Tao isn't conscious. I concede that a demonstration of artificial consciousness would falsify nondualism. However, future claims of artificial consciousness should be rejected if they only prove AI.

"Christianity has everything the West needs. We don't need nondualism."

I recognize the immense value of Christianity. However, not every Western mind is willing or able to make the supernatural assumptions required for the Christian faith. And there are other faiths as well. Since people of all faiths and no faith are destined to share tomorrow's world, how do we proceed?

As long as Christianity and other faiths are about religious, mind-independent matters and science and existential reason about mind-dependent matters, there is no need for religious people, nondualists, and scientists to have conflicts over their beliefs. This is the way of nondualistic existential reason.

"Eastern nondualism doesn't lead to more happiness than Western dualism. In Japan, the suicide rate is much higher than in the West."

I don't advocate an "Eastern" way of life but merely to recognize Eastern wisdom, learn from it, and combine it with our Western rational, individualistic tradition.

"China is nondualistic but not a free society. If we choose for nondualism, we will end up like China and lose our freedom."

If we cherish our freedom, we should understand what threatens it: utopian ideology instead of rational nondualism. Our success in remaining free societies that deliver on the promise of a good life to their citizens will be proportionate to our level of trust in reason and assertiveness on the international stage. Nondualism shows how to reconnect with our reasonable subjective interests and allows the West and China to deepen their equal partnership.

"Your insistence on rational solutions shows you are a populist because they don't work in the complex real world. Our fate is beyond our control."

Nondualism requires that our fate is not beyond our control. Inertia and irrational, intentionally divisive policies hit those hardest who need our help most. Complexity is a poor excuse for inaction.

And how committed to freedom and democracy are those who routinely disparage their opponents as populists? Their disdain doesn't make them look more "objective" but rather the opposite: more biased and demagogic. The rational law of identity of indiscernibles implies that the words democracy and populism identify the same substance if all their properties are equal. So, how *do* we tell populism from democracy? A lack of existential reason can perhaps expose populism.

"The author's thoughts are random because he goes all over the place. It seems that he has gone mad."

It's somewhat hard to defend myself against the accusation of madness because I probably wouldn't be aware of it. But let me try anyway. True nondualism connects the dots between the deepest personal, the utmost universal, and everything in between. This can give the impression of haphazardness. Admittedly, this book is also less structured than my previous ones—but thereby, hopefully, more accessible. And my perspectives may be unfamiliar to those unacquainted with Eastern thought.

However, I seek to be coherent and systematic in my arguments. They may contain inaccuracies because I am only human and don't mind learning about possible mistakes. It is merely the best I can do. But considering my arguments random and the product of a lost mind seems a typical Freudian psychological defense mechanism. Some critics are so unsettled by nonduality and their inability to understand it that they prefer to deal with it by sweeping rejection (denial) and externalizing their cognitive limitations (projection).

EPICURUS MEETS SAM HARRIS

"O, Sam Harris!"

"Epicurus. Pleasure!"

"The pleasure is all mine! Tell me, Sam, are you determined to eradicate superstition?"

"Yes I am, Epicurus."

"Should we stop reading a final purpose into our existence in the observable world because there is no evidence of divine intervention?"

"Spot on."

"Are we better off discovering the laws of nature than being afraid of the unknowable?"

"Of course! We are modern people, right? We have learned a thing or two."

"Do you consider that the key to our consciousness can be found in our body?"

"Correct, Epicurus. More specifically, it can be found in the brain. If we study it thoroughly, we can find scientific answers to psychological and even ethical questions."

"*Yes, I read something similar in your books. In your view, objective facts in the brain determine morality.*"

"They do. It's all science. Anything else is superstition."

"*But Sam, I don't understand. You also flirt with nondualism, even though you seem to compartmentalize that attitude and only apply it to spirituality.*"

"What do you mean?"

"*When you believe that objective facts in the brain determine our morality, you are outing yourself as a dualist. For true nondualists, objective facts are a contradiction in terms because objective means something separate from the mind. Moreover, the only logically consistent nondualistic account of the brain must be that the mind imagines the brain, not that the brain causes the mind. Otherwise, the immaterial mind is a dualistic entity separate from the material brain.*"

"I may need a moment to chew on that."

"*No problem, Sam. Nonduality is anyway more of the author's hobby horse than mine. I only support him insofar as we both fervently champion reason. And since you seem to be an implicit dualist, reason also leads me to suspect that you see* free will *as an illusion.*"

"I do believe it to be an illusion. But what's dualistic about that?"

"*Because if you believe that objective facts in the physical brain cause the mind, these objective facts will just mechanically tick on and on and determine one's behavior via the mind. A mind produced by the brain must be devoid of free will, even when it's under the illusion of having it. But suppose we reverse the metaphysical model and have the mind imagine the brain. In that case, the mind is free to discover and create its destiny even when we have to conclude that it was conceptually deterministic. Determinism and free will are only compatible if the mind is one with everything there is. The pivotal question is, do we* have *free will, as dualism leads us to believe, or* are *we free will, as nondualism implies?*"

"As a scientist, I only claim what can be verified."

"*Sam, since you are not a strict nondualist and believe that free will is an illusion, do you consider sinners just unlucky and badly informed people?*"

"I do, Epicurus."

4. THE NATURE OF OUR NONDUALITY

"All things considered, Sam, we are brothers in thought because I am an implicit dualist like you. Lao Tzu made that clear to me in the previous chapter. Like you, I believe that fearing the gods is superstitious because we are just a swarm of atoms swerving around in complex yet regular ways. And I believe that harmful desires rather than devilish spells make sinners sin. Our moral compasses merely need calibration through education. That is the humane way to think."

"Amen to that . . . uhm, I mean, I agree."

"O, Sam Harris, I championed the same causes as you do. In your time, my philosophy wouldn't encounter the resistance it did in the Western Christian tradition since it merely states that the human world and the divine, the natural and the supernatural, are separate and cannot be reasonably thought to influence one another. If the supernatural influences the natural, it is not supernatural anymore but nature itself. Are you a skeptic, Sam?"

"I am, in a scientific way."

"So, how do you distinguish knowledge from beliefs?"

"Through logic and verification."

"But as a philosopher, you know Hume's problem of induction. If you verify something today, it isn't necessarily true that you can verify it always, even when it is a sufficient reason to believe that you can. Does not all conceptual knowledge consist of beliefs? Aren't the a priori logical principles ultimately also empirical? Doesn't the nonduality you explore necessitate that everything in our minds is experience?"

"That might be true, but some beliefs are more rational and scientific than others."

"I agree—we can ensure our mind-dependent beliefs are rational and scientific and leave mind-independent beliefs to religion and fiction. This allows harmony between science and religion because they have separate turfs."

"Whoa! Not so fast, Epicurus. Non-overlapping magisteria . . . that's what Stephen Jay Gould proposed."

"Gould's theory is different. He suggests splitting the scientific and religious realms according to the classical dualistic criterion of objective facts versus subjective values."

"That may be true. But still, in practice, religion *does* intervene in mind-dependent matters. Deeply."

"Don't I know it. . . ."

". . . And not in a good way! Religion is a net liability, not an asset."

"If you say so."

"So why don't you do as I: simply state that God doesn't exist? Why aren't you an atheist?"

"That's a terrific question, Sam. I am agnostic: I claim we can't know if God exists. You are an atheist. You also claim we can't know if God exists, but you add that God does not exist. So, your belief in the inexistence of God is necessarily faith-based because it cannot be verified. Given your aversion to lying, what you say must also be what you believe. So, in the existential knowledge template, your belief in the inexistence of God is not rational—not mind-dependent, but mind-independent because it is a claim about the unknowable. Paradoxically, your atheism is a religious belief."

"O, Epicurus, you are certainly not the first to throw that one at me!"

"But what's wrong with the argument?"

"It's metaphysics. I am a scientist. I only claim what can be verified."

"And how do you verify the validity of that?"

". . ."

"Sam?"

"Come on, Epicurus, let's be objective here! Let me point out that some of the nondualists that you and I cozy up to do exactly the same as I do. Since we cannot possibly know reality according to the nondualists, we have to assume that it doesn't exist. I do the same with God as nondualists with reality."

"Indeed, if reality is one's god, as it is for dualistic scientists, then you have a good point."

"I subscribe to nondualism. But I also believe in the scientific quest for *the Ancient One*, as Einstein calls it, the overarching, mind-independent principle that governs the universe—so, indeed, reality. Even when we might never find it."

"Ah, Sam, but then you are a monistic dualist rather than a nondualist. You can't have your nondualistic cake and eat it."

"What's the difference?"

"Monistic dualists like you consider that science is about reality and spirituality about the oneness, the nonduality. They ignore that reality means something separate from the mind—something without a subject. Lao Tzu told me that dealing with such contradictions gives him a massive headache."

"I see. Maybe I am more of a scientist and atheist than a nondualist. But you seem reluctant to deny the existence of God. Let me tell you, in my time and place, it is perfectly acceptable and even quite popular to do so."

"Reason demands me to refrain from claims about the supernatural. And if we consider God natural instead, then we can know Her rationally. But I don't know enough about religion to discuss such an immanent God."

"Precisely my point, Epicurus! I grant you that true nondualists shouldn't claim any objective knowledge because reality implies something different from experience. But according to that argument, if God isn't supernatural, we should also not call Him God. The inconceivable but natural nonduality is known as Tao, and we could call it God as well, but that doesn't make sense because the connotations are entirely different. So, it's best to conclude that God is non-existent—or supernatural and not an entity to make reasonable claims about."

"You have convinced me, Sam. Your arguments are airtight. I may have become too much of an "a-realist," just like you are an atheist. Maybe I've hung out with the author of this book too much. Since God and reality are mind-independent, we'd better declare ourselves agnostic about both deities. This way, religious and scientific people can coexist harmoniously, as can nondualists and dualists."

"But why don't you deny God's existence?"

". . ."

"Epicurus?"

". . ."

The Zen Master

I was about to finish the book here. But this morning, I woke up from such a vivid dream that I felt it would make for a better ending. So let me share my dream.

I dreamt I went to a Buddhist monastery. I should clarify that I am not a Buddhist and never went to such a place or even thought about going there. I am fine with familiarizing myself with the teachings through books and other media. But maybe something inside me said I should ask for feedback from the masters about my spiritual and metaphysical tenets.

So, in my dream, I arrive at the monastery. There, I meet many aspiring Zen monks and talk with them. A young man. A middle-aged monk from another monastery. We take turns talking with the highest Zen master of the monastery. I come after these two gentlemen.

When it is my turn and I enter his room, I feel reverence for the master's charismatic and warm personality. We start our conversation. I don't remember what we spoke of, but I do remember that my genuine admiration is mixed with a mild skepticism I feel for all the people in the monastery. I speak respectfully with the master—but also with candor and confidence that might send him a different message than my respect.

We sit at a table with a small wooden cabinet on it. The master says he always tells his disciples a few of seven stories. The little cabinet contains seven wooden slates. The master takes out two. Each slate has a story written on it. He tells me these two stories, but I don't remember what they were about. He lets me react to the stories, then puts the slates back into the cabinet. He says, "Now I will tell you a third and last story, but you will not have a comeback for it." I feel a slight reproach in his voice.

I acknowledge and wait while the master picks the third slate from the cabinet. The master then looks me in the eyes

4. THE NATURE OF OUR NONDUALITY

and asks me, "Do you know what Zen Buddhism is all about?"

I tell him that I don't.

He says calmly, "Love."

His words and the implied reproach wound me. I try to defend myself: "I have written a lot about love and how it emanates from Tao!"

But the Zen master remains silent. And with surgical precision, his words find their way deep inside my heart and hit the spot I think the master was targeting. I remember again that I am not a master but still learning: a seeker who shares his progress with others.

In the last scene of my dream, I have rejoined the other disciples and some other masters. We are having a pleasant conversation. I feel distinctly low in the social hierarchy of this group, but that feels fine. Merely listening is enough. I feel markedly better now because I have found my place in the group, and we have become friends.

From my dream, I understand that even though I feel that I have grasped nondualistic metaphysics sufficiently to call myself enlightened—it would be cowardly not to—and am no longer a seeker but a finder this way, it is okay to still learn in other ways. I still regularly get deeper insights and learn more about sharing my understanding. I feel comfortable remaining a seeker and explorer in the world. Tao is there for all of us, but what it means to you and me is personal, can change and develop, and is even a matter of choice.

Fellow traveler, thank you for allowing me to join you on your journey and for joining me on mine. I offer you my friendship in return, no matter if we agree on worldly matters. We are all expressions of the same being and need each other to make sense of it. Even when you have found Tao and trust it to be your guide, you will also know that Tao, while giving the utmost clarity, is in itself a mystery. Tao is the mystery we share and know because it is the mystery we are.

And now is also the right moment to remember that Tao has an even greater treasure in store for us than clarity. A treasure to give and to receive.

Love.

ABOUT THE AUTHOR

Marcel Eschauzier, a Dutch native, is married and lives in Belgium. He used to travel a lot, working as a business consultant and living in different cultures. After a revealing experience in 2016, he shelved his suitcases to set out on the journey within and write about existential questions. As an engineer and philosophy aficionado, he is passionate about demystifying nonduality. He has a low social media profile and doesn't blog because he has a long-term perspective.
Marcel holds a Master of Science in Industrial Engineering and Management Science from the Eindhoven University of Technology in the Netherlands.

✺

Dear reader,

Thank you for reading this book. I hope you found it interesting. If you liked it and still have a moment to spare, would you please consider rating it on Amazon or Goodreads?
(The rating and review links resemble this:
amazon.com/review/create-review?&asin=B0C7DXRCJZ
and goodreads.com/book/show/175485044.)
Your appraisal is crucial for authors like me and helps other readers find books they might like. I also welcome your suggestions. You can reach me via the Facebook and LinkedIn pages below.
Thank you!

Marcel

Facebook.com/XRLMedia
LinkedIn.com/in/marceleschauzier
YouTube.com/@XRLMedia

Printed in Great Britain
by Amazon